People First:
The School Leader's Guide to Building & Cultivating Relationships with Teachers

Jennifer Hindman, Angela Seiders,
and Leslie Grant

LONDON AND NEW YORK

First published 2009 by Eye on Education

Published 2013 by Routledge
2 Park Square, Milton Park, Abingdon, Oxon OX14 4RN
711 Third Avenue, New York, NY, 10017, USA

Routledge is an imprint of the Taylor & Francis Group, an informa business

Copyright © 2009 Taylor & Francis

All rights reserved. No part of this book may be reprinted or reproduced or utilised in any form or by any electronic, mechanical, or other means, now known or hereafter invented, including photocopying and recording, or in any information storage or retrieval system, without permission in writing from the publishers.

Notices
No responsibility is assumed by the publisher for any injury and/or damage to persons or property as a matter of products liability, negligence or otherwise, or from any use of operation of any methods, products, instructions or ideas contained in the material herein.

Practitioners and researchers must always rely on their own experience and knowledge in evaluating and using any information, methods, compounds, or experiments described herein. In using such information or methods they should be mindful of their own safety and the safety of others, including parties for whom they have a professional responsibility.

Product or corporate names may be trademarks or registered trademarks, and are used only for identification and explanation without intent to infringe.

Library of Congress Cataloging-in-Publication Data
    Hindman, Jennifer L., 1971-
    People first : the school leader's guide to building & cultivating relationships with teachers / Jennifer Hindman, Angela Seiders, and Leslie Grant.
       p. cm.
    Includes bibliographical references.
    ISBN 978-1-59667-113-3
    1.Teacher-principal relationships.2.School management and organizations.3.Communication in education. I. Seiders, Angela. II. Grant, Leslie W., 1968- III.Title.
    LB2831.6H56 2008
    371.1'96—dc22
                                    2008044565

ISBN 13: 978-1-59667-113-3 (pbk)

Also Available from Eye On Education

**Motivating and Inspiring Teachers:
The Educational Leader's Guide for Building Staff Morale, 2nd Ed.**
Todd Whitaker, Beth Whitaker and Dale Lumpa

**The High-Trust Classroom:
Raising Achievement from the Inside Out**
Lonnie Moore

**Creating School Cultures That Embrace Learning:
What Successful Leaders Do**
Tony Thacker, John S. Bell and Franklin P. Schargel

Applying Servant Leadership in Today's Schools
Mary K. Culver

**Leadership Connectors:
Six Keys to Developing Relationships in Schools**
Phyllis Ann Hensley and LaVern Burmeister

Managing Conflict: 50 Strategies for School Leaders
Stacey Edmonson, Julie Combs and Sandra Harris

**Lead Me—I Dare You!
Managing Resistance to School Change**
Sherrel Bergmann and Judith Brough

Dealing with Difficult Teachers, 2nd Ed.
Todd Whitaker

**What Great Principals Do Differently:
15 Things That Matter Most**
Todd Whitaker

Get Organized! Time Management for School Leaders
Frank Buck

Lead With Me: A Principals's Guide to Teacher Leadership
Gayle Moller and Anita Pankake

Professional Development: What Works
Sally J. Zepeda

**Talk it Out!
The Educator's Guide to Successful Difficult Conversations**
Barbara E. Sanderson

This book is dedicated to

All the leaders who make the choice everyday to support the learning of students and work of the teachers with whom they work.

My children Miriam and Malachi whose education will benefit from leaders who cultivate relationships with their teachers
—JLH

My parents Mr. and Mrs. Harry L. Mulder, Jr. who always taught me to respect my teachers as a student and now as an administrator
—AMS

Ashby Kilgore, who taught me early on in my own professional development about the importance of relationships in leading people
—LWG

Table of Contents

Foreword ix
About the Authors xi
Preface xiii
        Overview of the Book xiii
        Focus on Two Words xiv
        Contents of the Book xv
        Organization of the Book xv
        Uses for This Book xvi
        Reflection Moment xvii
Acknowledgements xix

Chapter 1 Leadership Is About Relationships 1
        Consider Relationships as Gears 3
        Know Thyself 5
        Develop Relationships 6
        Be Credible 9
        Recap 10
        Reflection Moment 11

Chapter 2 Vision: Setting the Course 13
    Assess the Risk 15
    Determine Where To Go 18
    Undertake the Journey 23
    Are You There Yet? 27
    Reflect on the Process and Outcomes 27
    Recap 31
    Reflection Moment 31

Chapter 3 Communication: Compelling, Open, Crisp, and Clear 33
    Welcoming Environment 35
        Get to Know Folks 36
        Design Inviting Opportunities for Staff Interactions . . 41
    Productive Messages and Feedback 45
        Use Effective Techniques 46
        Avoid Pitfalls That Undermine Your Intent 51
        Show What Is Valued 54
    Recap 57
    Reflection Moment 57

Chapter 4 Team Sense: Choose Them Wisely, Use Them Wisely, or Lose Them Completely 59
    Wise Staffing Decisions 61
        Choose Teachers Deliberately, Not Out of Necessity 62
        Select the Lead Team 64
        Know Your People As You Assign Responsibilities . . 66
    Thoughtful Teacher Development Choices 67
        Have Your Staff Understand Each Other's Strengths and Weaknesses 68
        Create a Tradition with Leadership Development . . 72

	Contentious Retention Efforts	75
	Value Staff Input	76
	Share the Glory	78
	Recap	79
	Reflection Moment	80
Chapter 5	**Influence: Leaders Positively Affecting Teachers** . . .	81
	Respected Leadership	82
	Be Influential within Your Domain	83
	Demonstrate Influence Beyond	89
	Deliberate Decisions	92
	Consider the Ripple Effect	93
	Make Choices in the Best Interests of Students	95
	Concerted Efforts	97
	Be Visible	97
	Plan, Monitor, and Schedule	100
	Recap	102
	Reflection Moment	102
Chapter 6	**Conclusion: Relationships Matter.**	105
	Benefits and Challenges in Building Relationships . . .	105
	Validating Relationships	106
	Vision	107
	Communication	108
	Team Sense	109
	Influence	109
	Recap	110
References	. . . .	113

Foreword

Have you ever considered whether school is a happy place to be? Happiness is one of the most fundamentally important human aspirations: Governments attempt to legislate it, families support it, and individuals need it. And yet happiness may be one of the most neglected attributes of our schools. In our ongoing quest for academic excellence, higher student achievement, adequate yearly progress, and the like, let us not forget the value and validity of making schools good places to be.

In *People First: The School Leader's Guide to Building & Cultivating Relationships with Teachers*, Jennifer Hindman, Angela Seiders, and Leslie Grant set out to explore a key dimension of creating within our schools a positive environment and, by extension, a happier place to live and learn. The focus of the book, to a large extent, is the creation and nurturing of positive working relations.

If we take a macro view of school operations, *how* we work with one another is as indispensable as *what* work we do in order to help our schools flourish. This soft side of schooling—that is, the *how* we work together—can be so influential as to dictate the quality of teachers and staff we are able to attract and keep. Frederick Herzberg, in his theory of what motivates us and in subsequent studies related to his two-factor theory of motivation, described interpersonal relations with peers and supervisors as essential hygiene (or maintenance) factors that can lead to job dissatisfaction if not fulfilled (Hertzberg, 1966). When the working relationships are negative (rather than positive as advocated so well in this text), people become dismayed and even choose to leave the organization. Simply put, relationships matter.

Related to the importance of positive relationships and high quality teaching, Michael Fullan and colleagues found in a study of high-trust cultures in the Chicago Public Schools that in trusting school cultures there is more, not less, likelihood of taking action against persistently uncaring or incompetent teachers in order to protect the well-being of the school. In fact, they found that "failure to act can poison the whole atmosphere" (Fullan, Bertani, & Quinn, 2004, 45).

One need only to consider the key constructs that appear repeatedly throughout this book to understand the value the authors place on positiveness: good relationships, reflection, welcoming climate, thoughtfulness, team attributes, and the like. It is to this end—building and sustaining positive relationships in our schools—that Hindman, Seiders, and Grant have provided this valuable addition to the educational literature. I trust you find its conceptually sound and practical advice informative and influential in your own educational practice.

James H. Stronge

About the Authors

Jennifer L. Hindman, Ph.D., is an education consultant and writer. Her passion is making learning relevant as she connects the tacit knowledge with the research base. She is known for identifying with her audiences and for her ability to connect research to practice. She is the coauthor of *The Teacher Quality Index: A Protocol for Teacher Selection* (2006, ASCD) and *Handbook for Qualities of Effective Teachers* (2004, ASCD). She has been published in numerous state and national journals including the *Journal of Personnel Evaluation in Education, Principal Leadership,* and *Educational Leadership.* She is the former editor of *The Teacher Quality Digest.*

A former teacher and science specialist, Jennifer consults in the areas of effective teaching, employee evaluation, and teacher selection. She earned her doctorate in educational policy, planning, and leadership from The College of William and Mary. She can be reached at jennyhindman@cox.net.

Angela M. Seiders is a principal in the Newport News (Virginia) Public Schools. A former realtor, Angie began her education career as a middle school science teacher. As a teacher leader she worked as a science specialist and an instructional specialist in a K–8 setting. As a building-level administrator Angie has been an assistant principal, an instructional program administrator, and a principal. Twice recognized as the Middle Principal of the Year by her school system's Parent-Teacher Association, she seeks to connect the community and school. Additionally, she contributes to the profession through mentoring new principals and supporting the professional growth of others in her school and district. Angie has presented her work at state and national conferences such as the Southern Regional Education Board. She believes that all children can achieve academically through perseverance and their natural talents as their instruction is facilitated in nurturing classrooms and at home. She earned a master's degree in educational leadership from George Washington University. She can be reached at angela.seiders@nn.k12.va.us.

Leslie W. Grant, Ph.D., serves as Visiting Assistant Professor in the School of Education at The College of William and Mary where she teaches in the teacher preparation and leadership preparation programs. Leslie is the coauthor of *Teacher-made Assessments: How to Connect Curriculum, Instruction, and Student Learning* (Eye on Education, 2008), and co-author with James Stronge of *Student Achievement Goal Setting: Using Data to Improve Teaching and Learning* (Eye On Education, 2009). She is the contributing author to *Qualities of Effective Teachers*, 2nd ed. (ASCD, 2008), written by James H. Stronge. Leslie provides consulting services in the area of classroom assessment and effective teaching.

Leslie has been a teacher, an instructional leader, and a content editor and item writer for a major test publishing company. She earned her doctoral degree in educational policy, planning and leadership from The College of William and Mary. She can be reached at grant_leslie@cox.net.

Preface

Great schools grow when educators understand that the power of their leadership lies in the strength of their relationships.
  —Gordon Donaldson, 2007, p. 29

Overview of the Book

People First: The School Leader's Guide to Building & Cultivating Relationships with Teachers resonates at the heart of a school: the relationships of the people within the physical walls. Building "staff relationships are one of the hardest challenges" (Killion, 2005) that leaders in such positions as grade-level lead teachers, department chairs, specialists, principals, and assistant principals have. This book provides the reader with tools to build strong working relationships with staff and colleagues. In paying attention to the "soft" skills, other goals ranging from student achievement to staff retention are addressed.

A strong staff inevitably benefits students as there is a common collegial culture to address school goals, mission, and vision. This book provides readers with practices and research relating to building and cultivating interpersonal relationships among school staff. We know that good leaders make a tremendous impact on their schools through effective leadership of their faculty and staff who, in turn, work with the students. We also know that accountability issues often get attention, but in the final analysis a school is about people and their learning. Based on research and practice, we offer a book that will serve as a resource for instructional leaders as they create motivating and rewarding relationships with their staffs.

We know that being an instructional leader is not a short 8-hour work day. One of the authors is a principal in an urban school district, and she wanted a book that she realistically would read. Another author is a former lead teacher in a middle school who thought that sharing ideas would help keep others from reinventing the wheel when it came to relationship building. The final author depends on relationships as she interacts with supervising teachers and their student teachers in her capacity as a university professor. The book acknowledges the time constraints of busy administrators and teacher leaders through its use of quick research summaries linked to practical application. This concise book is designed for readers who want a quick reference to ideas and guidance about essential components of building and cultivating productive working relationships.

Focus on Two Words

When thinking about relationships, there are many words that can be applied to them such as *developing, maintaining, fostering, growing, establishing, creating, enhancing, improving,* and the list continues. The words building and cultivating are deliberate choices. Consider the dictionary definitions of each in how instructional leaders, from teacher leaders to central office personnel, work with teachers.

> **build** (bild), *v.t.*
> To increase and strengthen; to establish and preserve. To create.
> Webster's New Twentieth Century Dictionary Unabridged(2nd ed.), p. 238

The 20th-century definition of building is particularly apt for a 21st-century instructional leader. There are those relationships that must be created from the beginning as there is not a prior relationship between the parties. Once established, the people involved work to preserve the relationship. Other times a relationship needs to be reinforced. Increasing and strengthening relationships are vital for growth and risk taking. "In the most successful schools, teachers supported by administrators take initiative to improve schoolwide policies and programs, teaching and learning, and communication," (Danielson, 2007, p. 19).

cul · ti · vate ('k&l-t&-"vAt), *v.t.*
to improve by labor, care, or study

Merriam-Webster's Online Dictionary

Word usage changes over time. Thirty years ago, people used the word cultivate when talking about plants (e.g., soil preparation, growing plants); however, today the dictionary definition has been expanded to include the cited meaning. Whether we are talking about plants or people, both respond to care and attention. There are existing relationships that require cultivating; these relationships are desperate for improvement. Just as a plant can wilt and die, so can a relationship. Yet with care, effort, and sometimes a studying of the issues, a relationship can recover and thrive.

Contents of the Book

This book offers instructional leaders ways to enhance the interactions between staff members in a school. Relationships range from simple networking to full-blown collaboration. Some aspects of relationship building shared in this book may initially seem like gimmicks, but they can lead to more substantive and sustained relationships. As one of the authors emphasizes, a school staff is a family with whom building strong and authentic relationships is essential. Depending on your needs, you may find it beneficial to use the following one-sentence summaries to decide where to start reading.

Chapter 1 presents an analogy of relationships to gears in a discussion of the role of a school leader in building relationships and trust among the faculty.

Chapter 2 presents initial steps that leaders may take to establish and support relationships that work toward their vision.

Chapter 3 examines the value of communication in relationships.

Chapter 4 explores the human resources aspect of relationships through a leader's team sense.

Chapter 5 considers the leader's influence on others and on student learning.

Chapter 6 examines the challenges and benefits to relationships that serve as the foundation for the interactions that occur within the school walls.

Organization of the Book

People First: The School Leader's Guide to Building & Cultivating Relationships with Teachers focuses on developing strong working relationships between teachers and instructional leaders. Good administrators and teacher leaders constantly seek to create a supportive environment where staff and students are focused on learning. Each chapter begins with an introduction that frames why relationships are integral to an aspect of an instructional leader's work. Following the introduction is a graphic organizer of the themes and key ideas presented in the chapter. For each theme, two to five key ideas are presented along with associated research. The Ideas From the Field sections contain ideas from people in schools with whom we have worked as well as some of our personal practices related to the research presented in each section. In some cases, many folks have had similar ideas, and so we created a composite idea from the field. Originally, these ideas were presented to school faculty and staffs and conference participants as a series of "lifesavers" (as in the flotation device). Tried and true, these ideas have worked in practice, so they are shared with you. We hope that they spark ideas of what you can do in your school.

Each chapter concludes with a Recap of the key ideas as well as a Reflection Moment. During the reflection moment, consider the three to five bulleted questions as they reflect your current practices and thoughts after reading the chapter. If possible, act on one of your reflections during the next day or two in school. Some insights take more of an investment of time and energy than others, but some reflections can have immediate impact.

Uses for This Book

People First seeks to provide a resource to practitioners on how to create and sustain supportive working relationships. Further, this book provides tools that leaders can use to model how teachers in turn may interact with students, families, and colleagues. In education, we often reinvent the wheel. We hope that instead of inventing, readers will tailor the ideas offered here to fit the unique needs of their workplace. This book can be a valuable resource for the following:

- *Aspiring school leaders and early career administrators* who are seeking insight from others on what has worked well for them to build relationships with staffs who support learners
- *Building-level administrators* who need ways to engage their staff members in meaningful focused relationships
- *Instructional leaders* who are mentoring new administrators
- *Teacher leaders* who are actively leading departments and grade levels
- *Professional development specialists* who provide training on interpersonal relations
- *Education professors* who can use the practical examples from the field in their instruction

Reflection Moment

Take 3 to 5 minutes to think about the following questions.

- What are my strengths when it comes to building relationships?
- What do I want to get out of reading this book?
- Which one of the chapters summarized in the Contents of the Book section should I read first to get some immediate ideas to use based on my needs?

Acknowledgements

Before becoming a writer, I quickly skimmed and often overlooked the acknowledgement page and preface. Yet these two sections contain valuable insight into the authors' writing. The preface is a preview of the book. The acknowledgements provide an opportunity to recognize the significant contributions of others whose support helped the book progress.

Although a bit unusual, the first acknowledgement is due Angie Seiders, the book's coauthor. This book began as a series of conversations over many years between Angie Seiders and her staff as she developed their leadership capabilities. As her friend and colleague, I had many opportunities to hear her share work stories as she transformed herself from teacher to instructional specialist to assistant principal to principal. After Angie received positive feedback from conference presentations, she became increasingly aware that not everyone was getting the benefit of good relationships as 21st-century soft skills took a back seat to standards and testing. Her passion for students, staff, and school was evident, but she did not have time to write a book—or so she thought. Yet, amid the obligations and responsibilities of providing leadership in an urban school and being a wife, daughter, and mother to two elementary-age children, she reviewed every written word and shared field ideas. This book would not exist without the instructional leadership experiences, what makes a difference tacit knowledge, perseverance with students and staff, and charisma of Angie Seiders.

Throughout the writing of this book, we asked our colleagues to provide feedback on the chapters. In particular, we wanted the Ideas from the Field to resonate strongly with readers as ideas that they could implement. In addition, we sought an alignment between the research literature and the field ideas. Thank you to the following professionals who provided candid feedback and suggestions:

- Judy Mahler was Angie Seiders' and my first assistant principal. She modeled the importance of relationships (see the summary of Chapter 6 for an author's note about her) and provided support for our professional growth. She is now retired after a career as a teacher, building-level administrator, and central office administrator.
- Christine Hill, Ph.D., elementary school principal
- Felicia Barnett, middle school principal
- Richard Nichols, high school principal

I also thank Eve Ford, Judy McCollum, and Cathie West, who read and provided comments on early versions of the manuscript.

As the writing of the book came to a close, James Stronge, Ph.D., Heritage Professor, and Mary Vause, a graduate assistant, at The College of William and Mary, applied their constructively critical eyes to our work. Further, we greatly appreciate Dr. Stronge's writing the foreword, in which he succinctly notes the value of positive working relationships that make the workplace a happier and more productive setting.

Finally, the support of Bob Sickles and his team at Eye on Education is greatly appreciated, especially the efforts of copy editor Carol Rawleigh. Bob saw the potential in this book and gave us the opportunity to share it with you.

1
Leadership Is About Relationships

Relationships permeate every aspect of interactions with stakeholders—from school management to instruction. Effective instructional leaders set the course, monitor the pulse of the school, departments, and grade level staffs, and empower others to achieve goals. Effective leaders know that more can be accomplished through productive relationships.

Leaders build and rely upon their relationships with staff. They engage in deep discussions about teaching and learning, develop leadership capacity in others, recognize accomplishments, support staff, provide feedback, follow through on commitments, and earn respect (Dinham, 2005; Hallinger & Heck, 1998; Sparks, 2005). In a study of 38 faculties achieving outstanding results, principals were identified as an integral component to success because of their visible, approachable, trustworthy, and creative relationships with staff (Dinham). Leaders also recognize the delicate balance between building and maintaining good relationships and challenging staff to change and improve (Hallinger & Heck; Paglin, 2000). Having the ability to establish and grow positive relationships is a necessary facet of being a good leader.

Author's Tale

20% Gains in One Year Built on a Foundation of Effective Leadership and Relationships

When I first came to my lovely school, I was sent to bring up student achievement. I made an appointment with every teacher and staff member to come in my office and meet with me. I asked them three basic questions, however much more information was given. The questions were broad and likely inspired by my attendance at a Rick DuFour* conference session:

1. What makes this school great?
2. What do "I" as the principal need to know about this school?
3. What steps can we take together to make this an even better school?

I gave school T-shirts to the teachers at the meetings and requested that they wear them the first day of the teacher work week in August. We needed to raise the bar with instruction, teamwork, and relationships. So, I organized two meetings:

- a leadership retreat (e.g., administrators, department chairs) held off-site (before the teachers returned) to get to know each other further and to discuss the vision for the school and leadership goals for the coming year.
- school staff development for the teachers' first day back around the theme of "Raising the Bar." I called the physical education teacher and asked whether she could do an icebreaker activity with the staff on the first day back to school related to the theme of increasing student learning. She did a wonderful job and got folks involved.

During the staff development, I pointed out that we all have different talents and weaknesses. In order to reinforce the idea, I had every teacher complete a learning style survey. Then they broke into groups based on their learning styles. They had to design a school with their group in 10 minutes while I observed each group. When they were done, each group talked about their ideal school and of course "funnies" that go along with each group. Through this activity teachers acknowledged the following:

---

* Rick DuFour is an education consultant who is known for his professional learning communities presentations and writings.

(Cont'd.)

> **Author's Tale** *(Continued)*
>
> - We are all unique and talented in different ways.
> - We should appreciate instead of judging and ridiculing.
> - We need to help each other.
> - And most important, we are all on the same team
>
> We focused a lot on student learning as well. The single most important outcome of that morning session was knowing that we could work together as a team to help each other's strengths and weaknesses. As a school we complemented each other.
>
> After the school staff development, we went to the school-systemwide staff development held at a convention center where we were the only school staff who had matching shirts. Something so simple made us look so good. Our appearance said that we were together, in sync, and a unified team. I even had another principal come up and say, "Smooth move, Seiders."
>
> While I realize it takes more than T-shirts to bring a team together, we liked the positive attention we received. You see, our school was originally known in the school system as the "red-headed step child." I was not sure why, but I knew it was not good. That year we worked hard and played hard. We had a united vision and worked as a team toward it. Our school came up 20% in reading and math on the state standardized tests.

Consider Relationships as Gears

One way to visualize the critical components influencing the relationship that an instructional leader has with faculty and staff members is with a set of gears. When all is well, the gear system directs energy to get the work done, but there are times when the gears grind under stress and strain. To describe critical attributes of relationships, we used gears because of their oddly appropriate technical names and also because for a gear to work each component must touch the next. Leaders touch real people in order to realize real goals (see Figure 1-1, next page).

The crank is the vision that provides the initial energy input to get the gears moving. The first gear, known as the *driver*, is aptly named because effective and open communication is a necessary component of

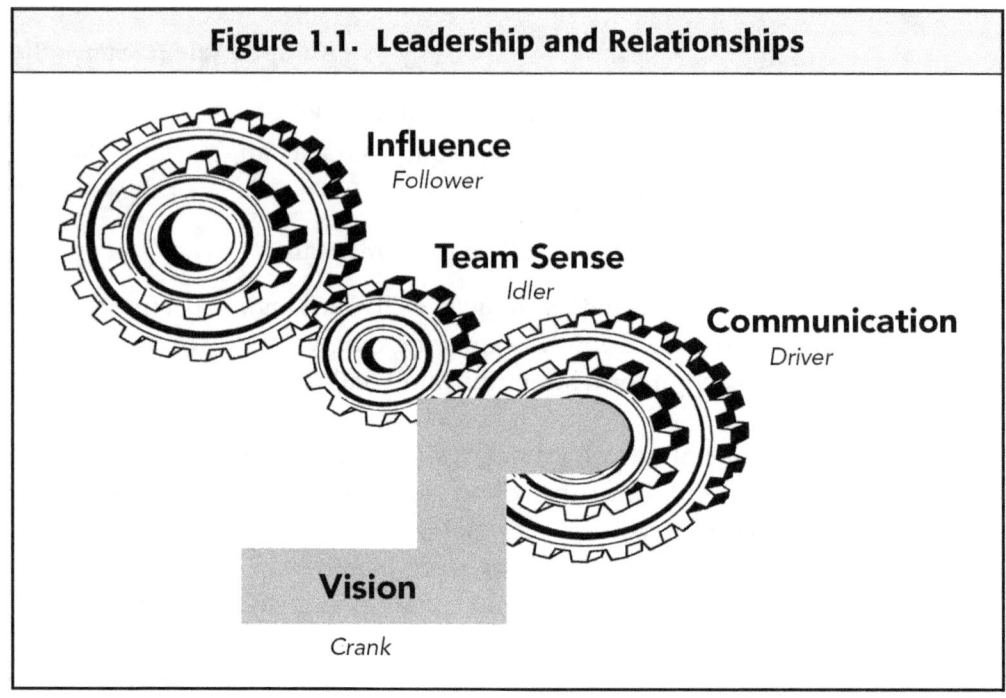

Figure 1.1. Leadership and Relationships

a relationship. The smaller middle gear called an *idler* represents team sense. The *follower* gear illustrates an instructional leader's influence for without a faculty and staff the vision is difficult to realize. Thus, the idler (team sense) rotates opposite the driver (communication) causing the follower (influence) to go the same direction as initially powered by the crank (vision). Effective leaders are aware of the inner workings of the organization and how individuals are likely to react. Chapters 2 through 5 delve deeper into each component. The following present each item in the gear analogy.

- *Vision* is the building block of a bridge between where a school is and where it wants to go (DuFour & Eaker, 1998). The vision is maintained by all, but may be initially powered by the leader (Huffman & Hipp, 2000).
- *Communication* is one means that faculty and staff use to determine if an administrator is credible, which is the first step to earning trust (Kouzes & Posner, 1993). Kouzes and Posner (2002) wrote that communication conveys characteristics such as honesty, forward thinking, inspiration, and competence.

- *Team sense* is the awareness that an instructional leader possesses of the relationship dynamics within the school, the structures that teams or groups of people assume, and the power of teams either to move an organization forward or to clog the efforts of others (Bolman and Deal, 1997). As World War II General George S. Patton is believed to have said, "Never tell people how to do things. Tell them what to do, and they will surprise you with their ingenuity."

- *Influence* is a powerful dynamic in relationship building. For an instructional leader to be effective, faculty and staff must accept his or her influence over the school, students, and themselves. An effective instructional leader's influence is about wielding power in a responsible and productive manner. Some leaders have influence without positional authority due to knowledge (Cohen & Bradford, 1990) as in the case of many teacher leaders.

Know Thyself

Leadership comes in many forms and depending on the theory to which one subscribes, the terms change. A leader's style may have both strengths and pitfalls, and once a leader becomes aware of these, he or she can choose to emphasize what works well and either improve or minimize what does not work as well. "Great man" theories posit leaders are born whereas behavioral theories say that leaders are made. In schools and central offices, two leadership theories seem to dominate with one focusing on the nuts and bolts of leadership and the other on the workers who fasten the nuts and bolts.

- Management or transactional theories—supervision, organization, and group performance are key tenets. Productive employees are rewarded and nonproductive employees are sanctioned.

- Relationship or transformational theories—focus is on the interaction between the leader and the followers. Leaders motivate and inspire both individual and group excellence (see gray box for one type of transformational leadership).

Studies have found that transformational leaders are able to support their followers in navigating the change process in order to bring sustained and desired outcomes (Dinham, 2005; Hallinger & Heck, 1998).

Entire books are written on leadership, and leadership style inventories abound. Knowing thyself is not about labeling your style of leadership with a name. Rather, it is acknowledging how you function as a leader. Leadership style affects the types of relationships that leaders have with their followers. Relationships are central in leadership and are used to establish influence. For example, in servant leadership there is a strong sense that people care about each other and that the leader is in service to them such that, "the school fully accepts its responsibility to do everything it can to care for the full range of needs of its students, teachers, and parents . . . it believes its academic responsibilities can be accomplished only through its stance of servant" (Sergiovanni, 1992, pp. 115–116). Effective instructional leaders know that the effectiveness of an organization is dependent upon the quality of the relationships within it.

> The term *servant leader* was coined by Robert Greenleaf to describe someone who chooses first to serve and then to lead.(1970). This style of leadership resonates well with people who understand that a group is stronger than an individual and that sharing power makes the organization and leader stronger. Servant leaders:
> - are transformational in that they awaken or capitalize on the best qualities within their followers (Farling, Stone, and Winston, 1999).
> - have an ability to influence people such that knowledge is shared, not bestowed (Buchen, 1998).
> - share the scarce resource of power as both a servant and a leader as they build relationships and look towards the future (Buchen).
> - listen to their faculty and staffs, look for the potential in them, and are honest (Lee & Zemke, 1993).

Develop Relationships

Relationships with high expectations as well as high levels of trust and support are characterized as high-quality relationships. Employees in high-quality relationships typically have higher job satisfaction, increased commitment to the organization, better communication with their leaders, and lower turnover than do their counterparts who have low-quality relationships (Harris & Kacmar, 2006; Truckenbrodt, 2000). Studies have found that employees' stress levels and turnover rates are lowest when employees have a moderate relationship (e.g., neither micromanaging nor uninvolved) with their leader (Morrow, Yoshinori, Crum, Ruben, & Pautsch, 2005; Truckenbrodt). The difference between the high and moderate level findings is likely due to the increased demand placed on high performing employees by their leaders.

Ideas from the Field

Call people by name. One of the simplest ways to enhance relationships is to know people's names and use them. This little action communicates that you know who that person is. If you are new to a school, look at last year's yearbook to help learn names in the building. Take team, grade level, or department photographs during the teacher work week preceding the start of school, label them with teachers' names, and post them in a common area for everyone's reference.

Consider how often you interact with each staff member. Perhaps take the faculty roster to reflect upon how you personally interact (e.g., one-to-one communication, such as a personal note, call, e-mail, or conversation—a faculty meeting doesn't count) with faculty members by writing a "D" next to those you communicate with nearly everyday, "W" for weekly, and "R" for rarely. Then put a star next to the names that you regularly call upon to perform extra duties, and place a check mark next to names where the teacher's performance is meeting expectations. Finally, review the list for trends in your interactions. Think about why you interact with someone a lot or rarely. It may be that one classroom is across from your office and another is out of the way, so geography is playing a role. However, if the reason is that a teacher is doing a fine job and there are fires to douse elsewhere, then make the effort to interact more with the professional.

Make interactions meaningful. Reflect on the quality of interactions with staff. Are they rushed? Do you listen attentively? Are you forthcoming if you do not have time for a conversation? Do you follow up with staff members when you say that you will? Show interest in what staff members are doing with students. If a staff member has shared a concern or sought assistance, make an effort to ask the teacher, "How's it going?"

Take time for staff relationships. In many school systems, dedicated "teacher-only" time without students during the contract period is often limited to a week before the first student day and a couple of hours a month for after-school meetings. Every minute is precious for communicating information, initiatives, and a host of other factoids. So consider how to build relationships while getting the "business of school" accomplished. Ask about dogs, children, or share funny stories based on what students may have said. For example, two girls on a field trip to Jamestown (the first permanent English settlement in North America) noticed feathers hanging in the air attached to a rope and one pointed and said, "There is a fan." To which the other little girl said, "I don't see the plug." If a teacher took a personal day to attend an out-of-town graduation of her son, ask about graduation when you see the teacher the next time. These little exchanges blending the personal and professional sides help make a person seem more accessible, which contributes to the building and cultivation of relationships.

Case in Point

A reading specialist kept homemade cookies in her office. When teachers came by to discuss student progress or receive support, they were assured of a tasty treat. Also, the specialist made a point to let folks know that they could always get cookies whether she was there or not; however, she took care to be in her office after school when folks frequently stopped by for an afternoon sugar boost. The cookies broke the ice for teachers who would just stop by to get a cookie and would wind up talking about instructional issues.

Please note any treat or incentive would work—cookies just happen to be what the reading specialist chose. Other lures have been a water cooler, freebies from area businesses who were changing over merchandise lines, stickers, bagel Friday, and the school's color printer (folks had to go in the media center to get print outs).

Determine if people know what you value. Tell several staff members that you are continuing to develop as a professional and you want to know how they perceive you. Specifically, you would like them to tell you three to five things that describe your work as their leader. The consistency or inconsistency of the responses is an indicator of how well people know you and what you value. Another indicator is how well the responses align to what you believe are the key facets of your work.

Be Credible

Credibility relates to the degree to which one believes that someone will do what he or she says. When a leader is new, attire, speech patterns, nonverbal communication, and physical appearance all contribute to how followers perceive the leader's credibility. Yet, when relationships have time to develop, past events are used to inform decisions on the credible nature of an individual. Kouzes and Posner (1993) conducted several leadership surveys starting in the 1980s. They determined that credibility was the foundation of leadership and relationships. Key qualities of highly credible leaders are commitment, pride, personal values in line with organizational goals, and team spirit (Kouzes & Posner). Further, good leaders know what is occurring in their school or departments because they are visible and approachable, talking to teachers, students, and other stakeholders (Dinham, 2005; Paglin, 2000). The relationship of the leader and the followers is essential in establishing credibility (Statt, 1994). By being visible and accessible, leaders can develop relationships and connect with staffs.

Ideas from the Field

Be current with the latest research. Being current in the field conveys that the leader is up-to-date with educational issues, approaches, and initiatives. A common response to "How much should a professional read in their area?" is to try and read one hour a day. The reality is carving out that time is tough. So work smarter, not harder by taking advantage of readily available research and education current event resources. For example, the PEN Weekly Newsblast (http://www.publiceducation.org/) is a free resource that arrives by e-mail on Friday summarizing education-related studies and topics from a variety of sources and at the end of each summary is a link to the actual article online. Carry education journals and other professional reading with you in the car and to appointments to read while waiting. Then e-mail information or put it in faculty members' boxes when an article of interest to that person is found.

Be visible. Bus lots, lunch duty, hallways, classrooms, faculty meetings, school system-mandated professional development, playgrounds, and a host of other job-related spaces are all places where a leader's presence communicates a message that you are available and that everyone is in the school united in their focus on the students. One principal used a notepad where the heading read, "Caught you being good" to leave positive messages in faculty members boxes. Of course being "out and about" also can alert a leader to areas that may need more monitoring and attention.

Value staff members' time. Leaders make the most of their faculty's and staffs' time. Make an effort to be on time. Be prepared for meetings with staff members. Resist the temptation to always contribute by taking time to listen and then respond if your response truly adds value—sometimes more is communicated by the affirmative head nod. Redesign the faculty meeting time slot, such that if a laundry list of issues and information can be covered by a memo, write it up, and use the remaining faculty meeting time as staff development on schoolwide initiative or for specific small group meetings such as vertical teaming. Continue to protect staff members from vendors and interest groups that want "just a few" minutes of faculty members' time by encouraging these folks to provide literature or to e-mail information to which faculty members can respond if they are interested. Finally, for those after hours or extra effort events, affirm to teachers that their time and contributions make a difference. After all, most teachers put in far more time than their contracts stipulate.

Recap

- Relationships are complex and integral to the effectiveness of leaders and their schools and departments.
- Vision, communication, team sense, and influence are relationship components.

- Leaders should critically examine their relationships with teachers.
- Transformational leaders get results through change embraced by stakeholders.
- Credibility is central to establishing and maintaining positive and productive relationships.

Reflection Moment

Take 3 to 5 minutes to think about the following questions.

- What am I doing as an instructional leader to communicate the value of relationships to the achievement of the school's vision?
- How do I establish relationships with new members to my faculty and staff?
- What do I do to maintain and nurture relationships with my stakeholders throughout the school year?
- Which one of the *Ideas from the Field* could I try this week? Use in the future?

2
Vision: Setting the Course

Ideally, vision is the focus of the school and something that everyone knows and embodies. If vision is not a part of the people, then it is, to paraphrase a colleague, like words written on a banner that could be ripped off the wall. Instructional leaders work toward a common vision with their faculty and staffs. Depending on the situation, an instructional leader such as a central office, content area supervisor may develop a vision and seek to cultivate it within departments spread throughout many school buildings. In other settings, the vision is collectively developed by those who will pursue it. Shared vision is powerful when it serves as the "bridge between the current reality of the school and what it hopes to become," (DuFour & Eaker, 1998, p. 84). For example, a study found that schools that were ready to become professional learning communities had shared leadership, shared vision, and strong communication and relationships, whereas schools that were not yet capable of supporting a learning community had reactive, rather than proactive, leaders and teachers who led only in the classroom (Huffman & Hipp, 2000). Vision can provide the fuel for success by setting a clear agenda for action, specifying what excellence and success are, and providing the direction for people to work proactively without heavy management (DuFour & Eaker, 1998).

Establishing common ground may be as simple as appealing to a common denominator or as challenging as having to bring adversarial parties together. Yet leaders know the inherent value of harnessing a group's capacity to move forward in a time when one individual cannot do it alone (Fullan, 2001). Colleagues and teachers are critical partners in the pursuit of a vision that results in student learning.

Motivated and energized leaders, faculty, and staff build relationships with each other, parents, and community members to create an environment that facilitates students' social and academic growth. Vision must permeate the actions of the people in the school. To that end, here are some key nonnegotiable facets to realizing a vision:

- All those who have a stake in the school must be well aware of the school's vision (DuFour & Eaker, 1998).
- The vision must be cultivated by the leader and maintained by all (Huffman & Hipp, 2000).
- All who come in contact with the vision need to understand their unique roles in owning it.
- Trust must exist among all involved in making the vision a reality.

A common vision brings groups together so that their efforts can then be focused on achieving the same targeted results. After all "isolation is the enemy of improvement" (Fullan, 2001, p. 130). Since schools are constantly working to improve in areas such as educational outcomes, student services, learning environments, and teacher growth, it is vital that leaders work with others to set a course for success.

Vision is the articulation of where potential seeks to become reality. Working towards a vision, involves work, change, and often the taking of strategic risks. Any time a change is made, there is the chance that the result will not be positive, hence the risk. Strategic denotes that something is important or required. So those choices that are necessary to bring about the desired change to work towards a vision are termed strategic risks. The team or leader determines that the strategic risk is necessary and worthwhile to accomplishing a goal or realizing a vision. Figure 2.1 provides an overview of the chapter, which differs from other chapters in that a process, rather than a series of related topics, is presented.

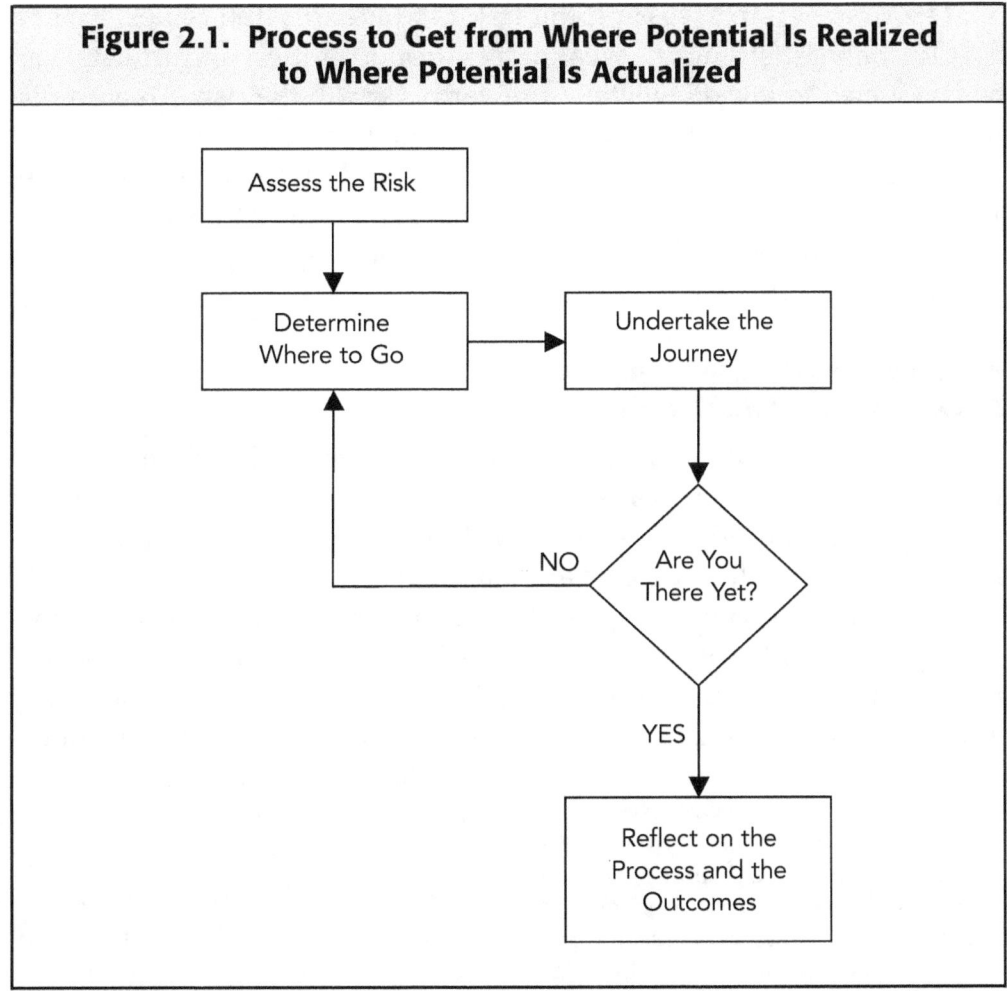

Figure 2.1. Process to Get from Where Potential Is Realized to Where Potential Is Actualized

Assess the Risk

What is the problem? What are possible solutions? Where are the hang-ups? Think of school leaders depicted in movies who took risks. For example, Principal Joe Clark, portrayed by Morgan Freeman in the movie *Lean on Me*, walked around the school with a baseball bat and a bullhorn. The tough love approach was aimed at getting despair and distraction out and success and learning in, and it worked. School leaders often take strategic risks so that students will reap the rewards. They may ensure student success by empowering teachers, changing the schedule, or a host of other actions.

The first step in assessing the risk is to identify the issues. Then a SWOT analysis (strengths, weaknesses, opportunities, and threats) can be conducted to decide whether a reward is worth the risk. An administrator or lead teacher then formulates actions to deal with threats and weaknesses and to capitalize on strengths and opportunities (Bryson, 1995). By knowing the terrain, educational leaders are in a better position to work with others to discuss and analyze the proposed change and the risk that accompanies it.

Ideas from the Field

Talk to your colleagues. (This idea from the field will be repeated four times, once under each subsection, since the chapter is framed as a process. Each time additional detail will be provided. A school-improvement-team plan will be used as an example.)

In discussions with colleagues, timing matters. When reviewing school testing data to identify issues that need to be addressed in the school improvement plan, resist the temptation to start planning immediately after the test results come back. The end of an academic year is an exhausting time; staff members have just completed draining rounds of testing, end-of-year grades and reports, and the conclusion of school activities. Take a break by scheduling a time near the beginning of school for a meeting with the lead team (see gray box) to review the test data and the previous year's school improvement plan. If possible have the conversation off-site, free from the distractions of the building. Ask colleagues to review and analyze their data prior to coming. Spend the day discussing, reflecting, and brainstorming. Emerge with a skeleton of the key issues.

> The term *lead team* is being used to identify a principal's formal leadership team. In a school setting, the term *administrative team* is often used to denote the principal and assistant principals. The term lead team broadens this application to include department heads, lead teachers, grade-level chairs, instructional specialists, the security chief, and other leaders in addition to the assistant principals.

Case in Point

A school principal, who just finished her first year, decided to have a lead team data day with her lead teachers the week after school got out and was upset because the teachers were tired and grumpy. They accomplished nothing during the day, and it was clearly not a good time.

In talking with an experienced colleague, the principal discerned that she had the right idea, but the timing made the execution off. It would have been better to take the teachers to a nice lunch and ask them some questions about the year in a more relaxed environment. The luncheon could have accomplished more brainstorming then the principal thought possible, if the principal came prepared to ask questions during the lunch to get the teachers thinking and reflecting for the next year. The time for a data day was not the end of the year, but rather a time after the lead team had recovered from the stress of ending a school year.

Find out what teachers perceive. An open-ended, end-of-the-year survey asking teachers about their perceptions of school needs, professional development needs, and areas for departmental improvement provides insight for leadership direction. A focus group is another option in which three to eight guiding questions are asked for discussion. It is vital that the administrator is open to hearing what is said. Another alternative is to have teachers complete a start/stop/continue form that will indicate what is working well and what may need to be changed.

Try ideas outside of the box. There was a time when block scheduling, inclusion, job-sharing, and a host of other education ideas were new. Thinking and acting outside of the box is an attribute of successful schools. When the ideas are based on sound reasoning, then try them. If an idea fails, then work with the professional to think about what could have been done differently and consider trying the idea again if appropriate. The key is to provide a supportive, professional environment rather than one in which professionals feel they cannot take strategic risks.

Case in Point

Building-level leadership decided that the current remediation schedule for middle schoolers was not good for the children because it took them from their physical education and elective time, and the current intervention was not working. There were 25 students in a grade level that needed remediation or an intervention for math and reading. The principal wanted to offer intervention, remediation, and enrichment classes. So she found 40 minutes in the day to do these classes. The beauty was that everyone taught during this period. All teachers, guidance counselors, librarians, and even teaching assistants helped out. This allowed the remediation classes to be 10 students or less, and meanwhile other students were involved in enrichment classes such as computer graphics, foreign language, career pathways, resume writing, creative writing, and so on.

Although all classes were successful, the entrepreneurship class went above and beyond. Barbara, the teacher, had the students study the economy, marketing plans, product designs, and budgeting, and she also had them write business proposals. Many professionals from the field came and spoke to the class. The students were asked to write an essay about why they wanted to be entrepreneurs. One speaker was so impressed that she flew 10 students to her company's headquarters where they participated in activities of the company. And yes, the principal did jump through hoops with the school board office to obtain permission.

Many opportunities in the school helped students learn to read and become better mathematicians, but this class provided opportunities that went beyond the students' expectations and prepared them for the real world. The small group, remediation-focused approach worked: Students' scores went up and more students obtained passing scores.

Determine Where to Go

From vision comes mission and from mission come goals... if only it were that simple and linear. For many leaders, the goals (e.g., district, school, grade level, departmental, professional) do indeed align to the mission and the vision, but there is more to the picture. In a U.S. study, researchers found that a lack of focus and clear priorities were challenges in low-performing schools that had many needs (Duke, Tucker, Salmonowicz, & Levy, 2007). Depending on the leadership structure of the school, direction may come from teacher groups, administration lead team, or the principal. Wherever the direction comes from, it needs to be consistent.

The vision and mission of any school should be about the students. In Figure 2.2, the vision, mission, goals, and actions of any school program ultimately reach the students. But in working toward a vision, leader reflection *and* teacher reflection are necessary, and these reflections should be shared in order to ensure that the vision is maintained. Thus, relationships are highly valued and essential for success (Huffman & Hipp; Richbell & Ratsiatou, 1999). These interpersonal relationships are especially valuable when risks are taken in order to enhance student success or when the going gets tough.

Effective leaders use higher order thinking skills to analyze and address problems by applying their knowledge of the school, students, and instruction (Krüger, Witziers, & Sleegers, 2007). Educational leaders discern where to focus efforts in a sea of competing needs and demands, an ability that is viewed by staff as a vital part of the work leaders do, according to a British study (Day, 2005). As one teacher in the study wrote, "he [principal] doesn't always bring into the school every new

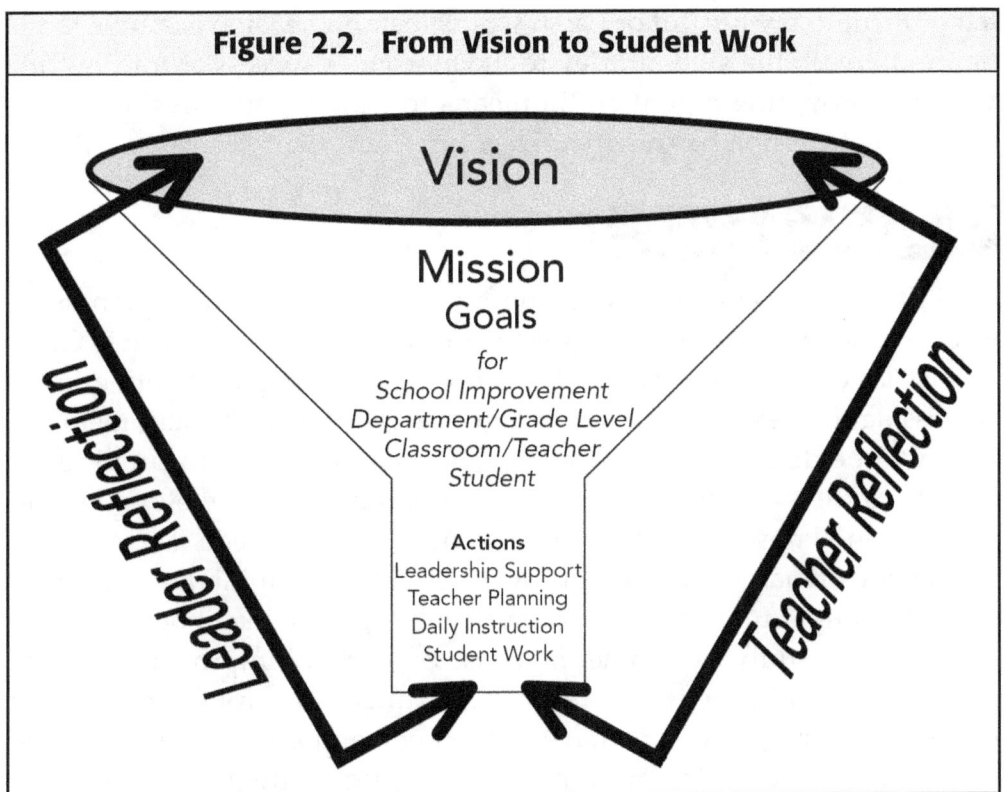

Figure 2.2. From Vision to Student Work

initiative. In some ways he fends things off, defends us against too much going on... we respect that," (Day, p. 277). Simply put, staff members need to know where to go—without roadblocks and constant detours.

Data analysis, listening to stakeholders, examining documents, and soliciting input help determine which strategies to pursue and where to apply resources. "A personal, well-integrated vision helps school leaders not only focus on the most important problems confronting them but also adopt and follow problem-solving strategies to effectively cope with the increased complexity of their work" (Krüger et al., 2007, p. 17). In essence, this is a vision, although it is not one that goes on a banner or a Web page. In a study about presidential rhetoric, charisma, and greatness, researchers suggested that leaders' ability to enact a vision is dependent upon their "ability to paint followers a verbal picture of what can be accomplished with their help," (Emrich, Brower, Feldman, & Garland, 2001, p. 527). Figure 2.3 uses a principal's opening-of-school remarks to illustrate four mediating processes of message delivery. The principal conveyed to listeners that they need to see beyond behavior that may tempt them to say hurtful or harsh words (comprehension example in the figure) to reach the student. Key to the message's success at transmitting vision is providing a goal and a means to act (last step in the figure); otherwise the vision has nowhere to go.

Ideas from the Field

Talk to your colleagues. Using a school improvement plan as an example, school leadership teams can often identify key issues. Goals and issues can also be discerned by informal leaders participating in the "assessing the risks" step (refer to Figure 2.1). Involve the staff members who will be doing much of the "on the ground" work to provide the muscle to the skeleton of issues. Teachers have well-developed skills, abilities, and knowledge of curriculum and students needs. They are also well aware of many of the threats or challenges to an initiative. Recognizing and thoughtfully addressing issues enhances the likelihood that they will be successfully overcome. In a case of a school improvement team, consider dividing the issues up by department, discipline, or support group in order to take advantage of teachers' and staff members' expertise. Listening to their opinions on promising strategies and research

	Figure 2.3. Getting Staff Support	
Mediating Process[a]	**Operation**	**Case in Point Example**
Attention	Get folks to listen to the message.	The principal wanted to raise awareness of the impact on students of negative messages from teachers. So she handed out photocopies of a picture of a child in which a blank circle replaced the child's face. Teachers held the picture as the meeting started.
Comprehension	Say the message so that it is easily understood. People can process concrete, verbal messages more easily than abstract ones.	The principal read anonymous statements that early arrivals to the meeting had told her in response to the question, "What, if any, unkind or hurtful words did a teacher say to you?"
Emotions	Provide a way to solicit a visceral response.	As the administrator read the statements (e.g.,"You will never amount to anything"; "You will never go to college"), the staff members crumpled the pieces of paper.
Memory and elaboration	Package the message so that listeners remember it when it is time to act.	The principal asked the teachers to picture an important child in their life (e.g., grandchild, nephew, daughter, family friend) and imagine that face in the blank space and asked them to smooth out the wrinkles. The wrinkles left from the unkind words could not be completely removed. A discussion of strategies to value students ensued. The administrator made the point that educators need to watch how they treat their students. What education professionals say and what they do could wrinkle students for life.

[a]Mediating processes were identified by Emrich, et al., 2001.

invests them in the process. This also gets faculty and staff on board with the work that needs to be done.

Case in Point

Physical education time was getting reduced across a school system's elementary schools in order to increase time for reading and math and to save money (since it allows two schools to share a physical education teacher). Since childhood obesity is a concern, the central office wanted teachers to infuse the core curriculum of math, reading, social studies, and science with movement. To ensure that this was accomplished, principals were required to make increased movement an item on the school improvement plan. Administrators in an overcrowded school knew this was going to be a significant challenge given that classrooms were crammed everywhere—one class was held in a converted textbook storage room, and two classes divided by a half wall met on the school stage and in its wings. They convened a study group consisting of the physical education teacher and teachers from each grade level to develop a plan that addressed the central office directive within the confines of the school. The result was a set schedule for the gym's usage on days when the physical education teacher was not at the school, identification of a series of instructional activities that could be done in the gym that involved movement, and a quick list of ways teachers could infuse activities with movement such as having students doing leg lunges to lunch or high stepping to the trash can. When administrators announced the scheduling change to the whole staff, the teachers from the study group presented strategies that were well received.

Examine your vision and mission statement. Do they accurately tell why your school exists? Vision and mission statements are used both internally and externally to promote organizational focus, define work efforts, and communicate. A vision statement may be created at the school district level, and often the statement alludes to what is done and what the future will hold, such as "ABC Public Schools prepares students to be critical-thinking, lifelong learners who are productive and responsible citizens and give back to their communities." Then at the school level, an individual mission statement is written that relates to the school district's vision.

Often school mission statements emphasize student instruction, a safe environment, and teaching excellence using a combination of means and ends, such as "123 Primary School is dedicated to *providing a nurturing, welcoming, challenging, engaging, appropriate, and safe learning environment* so that students can learn, teachers can teach, and families can participate in the education of students so that students have the **foundation** necessary for **future** school and **life success**." In the example, the italicized text shows the means (i.e., the items that the school and staff will do) and the bold text shows the ends (i.e., outcomes). The outcomes tell the purpose of the school.

Listen to others. Faculty and staffs have a vast amount of knowledge. Being open to hearing what they have to say about their school, students, and instruction supports informed decision making. Additionally, leaders should be flexible and respond to what they are hearing.

Align efforts. At the start of the chapter, Figure 2.2 illustrated how vision relates to student work, in essence how a group focus was funneled down to individual actions. The school needs teachers' work to successfully address items on the school improvement plan. Departments need teachers' work to achieve desired learning gains while supporting new teachers and a host of other obligations. Teachers have their own professional needs to meet, and if appropriate, a teacher's professional learning goal for staff development may be directly related to a school improvement goal. By using the vision to focus on students, professionals can overlay several goals to the current reality so that they know where their efforts intersect.

Undertake the Journey

Once a target has been established, work begins on getting there. In a study of the degree to which a school was prepared to support a professional learning community (e.g., high or low readiness), researchers found that in high-readiness schools there is a focus on students and achievement, and principals encourage teachers to initiate change, share responsibilities, and make decisions together that address a common vision. In contrast, in low-readiness schools, teachers and staff do not share a common vision (Huffman & Hipp, 2000). A book on organizational behavior (Newstrom & Davis, 1997) highlighted three common ways that people other than a leader may participate in the process:

1. On a consultative basis, which is brief and informative
2. As self-managed groups that have extensive control over the decision making and execution
3. Through quality circles, which involve a variety of people who can meet regularly and generate ideas for leadership to consider for implementation and subsequent evaluation. These circles provide an opportunity for teacher growth, recognition, and achievement while encouraging ownership of ideas.

As the journey continues, the vision "must be used to guide the daily operations and improvement initiatives of the school, and its importance must be communicated constantly," (DuFour & Eaker, 1998, p. 86).

Case in Point

An urban high school focused on a writing platform to promote the importance of having tools to succeed in all content areas. All instructional personnel were expected to infuse their curriculum with writing in authentic ways.

The writing specialist, known for her excellence in teaching and commitment to the writing process, was empowered to execute the school's focus. She was willing to model, advise, and coach individuals in navigating the writing process in their content areas. The formal message sent by the principal was backed up by the energy of this individual. People knew how hard the specialist worked and were often willing to do things for her because of their respect for her and positive relationship with her.

Teachers who were reluctant to use writing in their classes were mentored through the assignment by other members in the content areas. Peer pressure to perform also encouraged implementation. The teachers used different types of writing in the classroom and focus on the processes of prewriting, organizing, writing, editing, and rewriting.

The decision had positive results and resulted in a schoolwide focus on writing. Student test scores showed that the children became more solid writers. The principal's unwavering support of the infusion of writing into the curriculum and the review of biannual portfolios effectively created a culture of writing at the school. The portfolio expectations were to set goals at the start of the semester, to document and provide samples of diverse writing assignments, and to reflect individually and as a team on the success of meeting the writing goals. The two-way communication in the portfolio review meetings included praise, constructive criticisms, and discussion of how goals were or were not attained. The writing specialist, administration, and all teachers in the building undertook the challenge to improve writing.

Ideas from the Field

Talk to your colleagues. The way that a message is articulated matters in gaining support. Consider the following two ways that an instructional leader may introduce a strategy to the faculty:

- "I want you to *understand* how differentiated instruction can enhance student learning, so you can *think* about it in your classroom."

- "I want you to *see* how differentiated instruction can enhance student learning, so you can *imagine* it in your classroom."

The two statements are nearly identical except for two words. The first statement uses concept-based words: *understand* and *think*. While the second statement uses image-based words: *see* and *imagine*. A subtle change makes the second message more engaging so that listeners are more likely to respond. So to begin a dialogue with faculty in order to solicit their support and input, consider how a topic is framed.

Create opportunity for focused dialogue. Data reviews are meetings between teachers, an administrator, and a teacher leader (e.g., department/grade-level chair, specialist) in which student work or test data is reviewed. Teachers come to the meeting knowing that this will be a collegial dialogue about what is occurring in their classrooms. For example, predictor test data or writing portfolios may be reviewed. Teachers share what strategies they have found most effective and what has not worked so well. They share opinions and ideas about student progress. Whereas student groups may be discussed, putting names to the students personalizes and focuses the discussion. It is also an opportunity to say, "Darnell has made incredible growth this quarter as..." Likewise, if Tamra is struggling, the meeting participants can suggest ways to support her learning.

Just as students have warm-up activities at the start of class, faculty and department meetings can start with a discussion of an article or issue that was e-mailed prior to the meeting. Identify 10 articles at the start of the school year and ensure that staff has access to them (PDF, hardcopy) so teachers know what they need to prepare for a meeting. Administrators, teacher leaders, and teachers can discuss the research and apply it to the student population and to what is good for the school. If there is a systemwide in-service with lunch, secure a series of classrooms so that the staff can eat together and discuss the professional development that occurred in the morning relevant to their contexts. Place copies of timely articles in the faculty lounge or posted in the copier room for folks to read so that the topics can become the source of a spontaneous conversation or inquiry.

Use a timed agenda. A planned meeting should have an agenda. If there are several items to discuss, an agenda that suggests times for discussing each item provides boundaries and ensures that each item receives some attention during the allotted meeting time. Some issues will undoubtedly need another meeting or more time, and others can be handily addressed. This way backlogs are avoided, participants know their opportunity will come (even if they are at the bottom of the meeting time), and certain issues do not hijack the meeting. The timed agenda can be used as the reason for saying, "I am going to move this meeting along, and we will come back to this issue at another meeting." It also helps participants gauge their involvement, and even long-winded colleagues learn to quickly get to the point.

Monitor, monitor, monitor, and provide feedback. Walking around the building and briefly stopping in classrooms, the school leader learns what is taking place in the classroom. Consider leaving brief notes to the teacher about positives that were seen. These unplanned and informal drop-ins can also alert an administrator to problem areas that need to be addressed. Reviewing other data sources and offering comments is another way to maintain your finger on the pulse of the school, department, or grade level.

Are You There Yet?

In the process depicted in Figure 2.1, a question is asked, "Are you there yet?" This question is meant to direct the user to the next step in the process, whether it be revisiting a previous step or continuing to the final step. To answer the question, school leaders may be reviewing data, thinking about what changes they have seen in the school, talking to faculty, or considering a host of other sources.

The answer, is simply "yes" or "no," you are either at your destination or you are not. If the answer is yes, then advance to the next step in the process. If the answer is no, just know that sometimes there are detours that require re-evaluating where you want to go which will alter the next step of the journey that is undertaken. Oftentimes though, the desired destination is still the same, but the journey requires more time, additional resources, or different strategies. So ask the question and continue the process.

Reflect on the Process and Outcomes

To go forward, one needs to look backward every now and again. Sometimes this is called hindsight, reflection, or debriefing, yet no matter what the process is called, it is about examining the journey. When the process is rocky, effective leaders expend mental energy thinking about how to smooth out the road. They analyze what has occurred and consider what needs to happen. They seek input from other sources, including knowledgeable staff members, mentors, and experts in the field. Yet when an initiative is successful, leaders may not look back to identify what elements contributed to the success. Throughout the rest of this section, the example will use an elementary school principal, but the process of examining actions, data, and standards works regardless of position.

Sometimes a leader's prior experiences or lack thereof influences the process and subsequent outcomes. A study examined the background and actions of four principals and the results of their Grade 2 student performance on the Comprehensive Test of Basic Skills. Figure 2.4 shows the principals' actions and the students' results as each principal took an active role in the implementation of a new reading program (Mackey, Pitcher, & Decman, 2006). In using the results on Figure 2.4, one should recognize that three different groups of second graders took the test, so some variation is due to the fact that different students were tested each year. Nonetheless, some interesting reflections are possible.

Granted, a research article cannot answer all the questions, but it does provide a common basis for reflection as an outsider looking in. Certainly Principal No. 4 had an advantage due to a background in reading. That principal's school experienced the most success, and the principal was invested in the reading process as well as the program's implementation and monitoring. The other three principals relied heavily on others to execute the program. In the situation of Principals No. 1 and No. 3, the individuals to whom they delegated authority achieved positive results the year of the study. Yet, in the following year when the principals' actions were not the subject of a study, the percentile rankings declined. One could hypothesize that the principal's support combined with the efforts of individuals resulted in the one year increase. The scores for Principal No. 2 are perplexing as they dropped between years 1 and 2 and then remained flat for year 3. When Principal No. 4's actions showed strong support for the reading program, the initial gains in scores were sustained the next year.

When reflecting upon progress and outcomes, it can be helpful to compare the results with the school's goals, professional standards, evaluation standards, or your own internal knowledge. To continue with the example in Figure 2.4, the Interstate School Leaders Licensure Consortium (ISLLC) Standards all begin with the phrase, "A school administrator is an educational leader who promotes the success of all students," (Council of Chief State School Officers, CCSSO, 2008, p. 2). The first standard continues to indicate that an educational leader will promote student success "by facilitating the development, articulation, implementation, and stewardship of a vision of learning that is shared and supported by the school community," (CCSSO, p. 2). The principal whose school was most successful in the study summarized in Figure 2.4 embodied that standard, which has numerous functions including developing a positive culture of trust and collaboration, creating a strong curricular program,

Figure 2.4. Principal's Actions Resulting in Varying Levels of Student Achievement

Principal's Background	Actions	Results *Percentile Rank on the 2nd Grade Comprehensive Test of Basic Skills*		
		Year 1 *Before the study*	Year 2 *Study year*	Year 3 *Year after the study*
1 Speech Pathologist	◆ Chose the reading program after visiting other schools ◆ Invested in consultants to work onsite with teachers ◆ Relied on consultants to share the vision	30th	39th	35th
2 M. Ed. in clinical psychology	◆ Acted upon the reading specialists' recommendations ◆ Supported the vision by providing resources	51st	46th	46th
3 No degree listed 3 years as a teacher, 1 year as an assistant principal	◆ Accepted the central office recommendation for a reading program ◆ Relied upon consultants and a master teacher to execute the program ◆ Sought support of the master teacher to explain how the reading program worked	30th	50th	35th
4 M.Ed. in reading and working on an Ed.D.	◆ Articulated the vision to the staff ◆ Led professional development sessions ◆ Monitored the reading program	35th	55th	55th

Note: Data from Mackey, B., Pitcher, S., & Decman, J. (2006). The influence of four elementary principals upon their schools' reading programs and students' reading scores. *Education,* 127(1), 39–55. Retrieved April 24, 2008, from Academic Search Premier database.

supervising instruction, monitoring programs, and developing capacity of staff. The principals whose schools showed less growth were missing one or more of the essential functions defined by ISLLC. In order to grow and improve, these principals should implement one or more of the key components.

Ideas from the Field

Talk to your colleagues. Brainstorm constantly about what is working, what could be working better, what resources are needed, and how students are progressing. Talking about what is occurring in the school, in the classrooms, and in the lives of our students and teachers helps us reflect and adjust, and it also allows us to celebrate gains and address needs.

Case in Point—Refocusing Efforts

Sixth-grade mathematics students were struggling in the second half of the school year. A review of the data showed that the majority of students were indeed in need of help, but their needs were in a variety of areas. During a math department brainstorming session, the eighth-grade teachers who had planning time during the sixth-grade math block offered to go in during their planning time and support instruction. Teachers divided up students based on content knowledge needs and then provided focused skill remediation. Students who were not in need of support worked with the technology specialist and an assistant in the computer lab. This brief, time-intensive small group instruction worked, putting the students back on track.

Case in Point—Celebration

A high school ushered in a series of instructional strategies for schoolwide use. Training was provided and administrators checked submitted lesson plans to make sure that appropriate strategies were included. About midway through the school year, the principal noticed that several of the strategies were jelling and being used effectively. He took pictures of educators teaching and students working, and he documented effective hallway displays and student work samples. Then, using a slide show of the images set to the song "That's the Way I Like It" by KC and the Sunshine Band, the principal spoke about all of the positive developments in the school.

Be prepared to change midstream if necessary. By having open dialogue and continuing to examine the process, opportunities exist to change or revise a plan if an idea or approach does not turn out as well as one had anticipated. Some may persevere, but to borrow a quote credited to Albert Einstein, "Insanity is doing the same thing over and over again and expecting different results." If the data or anecdotal reports are not supporting the initiative, weigh the value of continuing against trying another alternative. As a leader, you may need to say to the group, "Your efforts were valiant, yet something different is needed." Then either provide direction or opportunity for the group to refocus. The decision about which course to take should be based on the capacity and mindset of your followers.

Make reflection deliberate. As a leader, you should set aside time to think about what you are doing professionally, answer questions to gauge progress, record thoughts and analysis, and review information from start to finish. This may take place in a car ride home, in the quiet of the early morning at your desk, or somewhere else. Continually examine your actions and the outcomes of those actions.

Recap

- Vision is a guiding light by which leaders focus their efforts, resources, and work of their staffs.
- Taking strategic risks is often necessary to attain desired outcomes when working toward a vision.
- Vision, mission, and goals provide a common language for a group of professionals whether they are at the school, department, or grade level.

Reflection Moment

Take 5 to 8 minutes to think about the following questions.

- What is my organization's vision?
- What is the mission for my domain of responsibility (e.g., school, department)?

- Remembering the last staff meeting, how did I communicate the vision for _____ (e.g., school, department) in terms of what I said and did?
- What strategic risks have I taken to support my staff working towards the organization's vision?
- Which one of the *Ideas from the Field* could I try this week? Use in the future?

3

Communication: Compelling, Open, Crisp, and Clear

Outstanding communication is a skill of highly effective leaders. The skills to communicate with ease can have a tremendous affect on a school or school district. Think about it—administrators must communicate effectively at all levels. They must work with teachers, staff, students, parents, and central office folks as well as the community. They must have the finesse to work well with all the stakeholders who contribute to a quality education for children. So how does that happen? How do you communicate when change needs to take place? How do you communicate to your staff, students, and community that you have the best educational program?

Some leaders are better communicators than others. Some leaders have to work harder to have compelling, open, crisp, and clear communication. There are speakers who make introductions and closing speeches appear effortless and seem to connect with everyone in the room. The mannerisms and phrases used by instructional leaders and department chairs to communicate to faculty can convey confidence and competence in the message being delivered. For example, an instructional mathematics coach may field questions on a variety of topics from assessment to planning for mathematics instruction, rapidly giving well-formed and informed responses. The reality is that "communication is an important process inside schools and the most frequently used tool by organizational leaders" (Ärlestig, 2007, p. 262).

Communicating vital information face-to-face is invaluable as the most efficient way of communicating information with high quality (Smith, 2001). Yet the dynamic reality of working in schools necessitates communicating with a variety of methods, including, but not limited to, e-mail, text-messaging, intercom announcements, internal television programming, telephone, and memos. The tools used to convey messages when face-to-face exchanges are not possible need consideration in a school district setting. Some schools have individual teacher voice mail, while others have one main phone line into the main office where messages do not always reach the teacher quickly. In some schools e-mail is available in the classroom, while others only have computer labs. A leader needs to assess the means for communication and use the avenues most likely to reach the stakeholders. Effective communication is essential to distribute information, forge collaborative relationships, make an impression, and work with people in general.

Whether working in the capacity of a central office administrator, building-level administrator, or teacher leader, one needs to articulate a commitment to the teachers with whom one is working. A reciprocal agreement needs to be reached so that individuals are connected to the big picture and do not experience the out-of-sight/out-of-mind sensation. Five basic components of communication are commitment, trust, time, language, and tools (Smith, 2001). Getting to know faculty and staff to establish a working relationship helps to establish trust. Engendering commitment and trust makes listeners receptive to the message. The remaining three components (i.e., timing, language, tools) enhance the effectiveness of the communication. Figure 3.1 provides an overview of the chapter which is divided into two main sections focused upon workplace interactions and effective exchange of information.

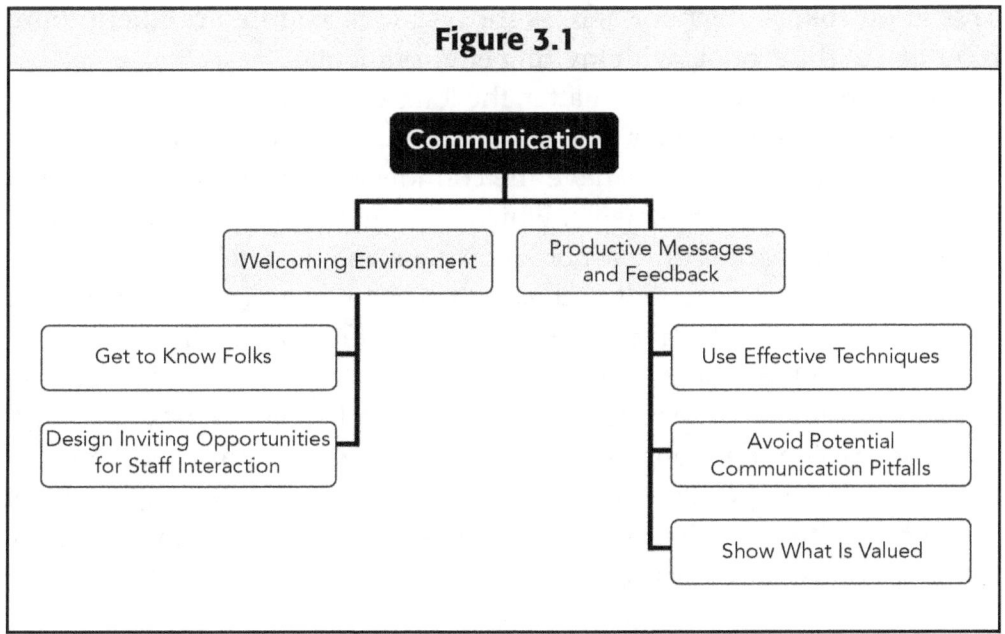

Figure 3.1

Welcoming Environment

Where would you rather wait, the Department of Motor Vehicles office with its lines, hard plastic seats, and electronic numbers or the doctor's office with plants, magazines, plastic covered cushioned chairs, and sick people? Neither place is high on a list to visit, but the doctor's office is a more welcoming environment because, it attempts of make people feel comfortable.

A welcoming environment is like a good first impression; it puts people at ease. People make judgments within the first 4 minutes of an encounter, and the impression typically is based upon:

- What is said—content (7%)?
- How what is said sounds—vocal quality (38%)
- Nonverbal communication—facial expression (55%) (Mehrabian, 1981)

Every person in the school has the opportunity to create a welcoming environment. The three bullets above can be applied to a welcoming environment. As leaders, we need to pay attention to what the environment says about us as a school and as individuals. People are likely more receptive to the schools with inviting environments.

While initial impressions matter, the long-term assessment by teachers that an instructional leader walks the talk—to borrow an old phrase—is critical. Educational leaders have the confidence to embrace educational missions and vision statements, which are big and lofty. They use them to guide their work with teachers who construct isolated informational facts into meaningful, connected experiences to be accessed by learners. When leaders are effective communicators, staffs are likely to identify strongly with the vision, mission, and organization. When leaders are poor communicators, employees are likely to become dissatisfied and may even resign their jobs (Madlock, 2008). So what is said and how it is delivered matters. Nonverbal and verbal communication lets stakeholders judge credibility, facilitates trust, and lets stakeholders know that they are a welcomed part of the educational process.

Get to Know Folks

What a simple idea—get to know the people with whom you work. Create situations in which coworkers can learn about each other. This sense of community will strengthens teachers' identification with the school, colleagues, and leadership (Ärlestig, 2007). Begin with positive communication and build rapport. Take advantage of opportunities to get to know all your stakeholders.

Ideas from the Field

Extend an invitation to know the school and you better. An administrator interviews a teacher applicant and recommends that the applicant receive a job offer. The administrator makes a phone call that evening (even though human resources may take time to generate the contract) and compliments the applicant on some aspect from the interview and asks whether he or she has any other questions about the school, the city, and so forth, thereby continuing to build a relationship. The administrator does not offer the applicant a job, as that is the responsibility of human resources. The next day, the department chair, who participated in the interview, calls and asks whether the applicant has any questions. These phone calls keep the communication open.

People often want to know more about the supervisor or ask questions that they were hesitant to ask in the interview. This way the teacher leader also builds a relationship with the interviewee as well. Once the applicant signs the contract, another call is made to ask the applicant to lunch and to see if she or he needs information about the local area. A welcome packet is sent from the school.

In between interviewing and hiring, the individual had two contacts by two separate individuals. After the hire, an additional contact was made. By having different individuals extend a welcoming hand, the applicant, now the new staff member, will have been introduced to several people invested in the school and in her or his success. This will help with relationships, communication, and making the person feel welcome and at ease for this new beginning.

Use conversation starters. Whether icebreakers centered on faculty trivia, discussion starters based on educational issues, needs, or developments, conversation starters are ideal for letting everyone have an opportunity to voice their thoughts and knowledge about a topic. These work the same as warm-up activities in classrooms when used as folks are arriving before the start of a faculty meeting. The discussion starters could be posted so that teachers can begin discussing the topics. Then have a quick way to share the information or show how the information ties into the meeting.

Case in Point

Faculty Guess Who is a fun way to get staff talking during teacher back-to-school week. Simply e-mail a request for faculty members to share something that fellow staff members may not know about them, such as their favorite book or movie, or perhaps ask teachers to tell what their favorite activity is when they are not teaching. Faculty Guess Who could be instructionally based such as a favorite concept to teach or something that the person does well and could share. The questions then can be published. Each staff member could be represented by a question: Who is the former mayor of Kokomo, Indiana? Who was Dustin Hoffman's personal assistant? Who was Miss Idaho? and, Who has taught for 22 years in the same classroom? The answers can be shared in a variety of formats from simply posting them to letting folks write in answers on a poster-sized sheet in the faculty lounge.

Mentor for success. Have expectations for mentors and their new teachers shared and discussed at a working lunch or afternoon break with food. (Mentors should already have been briefed on the expectations prior to agreeing to serve as mentors.) An example of an expectation for a teacher new to the profession may be to work with the mentor teacher to develop a long range set of plans for the year and daily lesson plans for the first two weeks of school—all before school starts. Then weekly (at a minimum), the mentor and teacher meet to review the upcoming week's plans and reflect on the previous week. An experienced teacher, who is merely new to the school system, may do collaborative planning with the mentor. Throughout the year, different mentor-teacher activities can be planned.

Some tips for starting off the school year organized for mentors and new teachers are to:

- Have an agenda for the new teacher orientation week.
- Plan some specific activities, if applicable, for teachers who are merely new to the school system as their mentoring needs are different from those who are new to the profession.
- Provide an opportunity for lead teachers to work with their new teachers both during orientation week and throughout the school year.
- Designate time for teachers to meet and interact with school support personnel such as the technology specialist, media/library specialist, counselors, custodians, and secretaries so that names, faces, and jobs become familiar.

Many schools and school systems have a mentor process in place for new teachers; however, mentoring is beneficial to veteran educators as well. Supporting others in navigating new situations and addressing challenges is a meaningful investment by a leader. For example, a principal may meet daily with assistant principals and key educational support professionals. A department head may meet weekly with teachers who are new to a particular class preparation to discuss lesson plans. A writing specialist may work with content area teachers to model and mentor writing across the curriculum.

Case in Point

Sometimes the best of planned routes requires a detour to an alternate destination due to the driving conditions. An elementary school with a staff size of 25 got 10 new teachers in one year. Of the 10 new teachers, 5 had previous teaching experience. The veteran teachers mobilized in the first week of school to support their new colleagues. Mentoring for teachers who were new to the profession and mentoring for simply new to the school began. Nine of the 10 new teachers thrived.

So, let's focus on the one remaining new teacher. During the teacher work week before school started, the fourth-grade-level chair became concerned about a new teacher whom we will call Jane Doe. Jane's views on the role of a teacher were out of touch with the reality of the profession. By the end of the second week of school, Jane's mentor, the two other fourth grade teachers and the grade-level chair had independently said something to the principal about Ms. Doe. The school invested significant energy in working with this fledging teacher. Jane observed expert teachers who modeled lessons during to one class so that she could teach another class the same lesson while the teacher observed, after which the two teachers would talk. Her mentor teacher and grade-level chair worked with her on the nuts and bolts of teaching from lesson planning to communication with families. Over the course of the several weeks, Jane participated in difficult conversations with her principal and her mentor, examining her teaching practices and her beliefs about teaching.

Sometimes as educators we want everyone to be happy and make no waves. Yet in the age of accountability, we can no longer hide things under the rug. We all know that students suffer when vital issues are deliberately ignored. It would have been easy for the school leadership to chalk Jane's issues up to first-year teacher rough spots, but her problems were significant. Jane was an energy drain on the teachers who tried to help her, ineffective in the classroom, and in general a nightmare for students and their families. There was no happy ending for Jane, who did not finish out the school year. For her former students, the silver lining came in the form of a dynamic, engaging, and competent teacher who was hired to replace Ms. Doe.

Change meeting sites. If the meeting is a grade-level or department-level meeting, alternate the classrooms in which the meetings are held. This way fellow teachers can see how colleagues organize their learning environments. During meetings, attention and eyes wander, so colleagues have an opportunity to notice classroom elements that they may not notice when rushing to ask a question during a planning period. A teacher may ask another teacher about the word wall used in a middle school science classroom or about the magnetic lunch/attendance count used to maximize instructional time. Meeting in different rooms begins to break down barriers that contribute to the teaching in isolation perception.

For larger meetings such as faculty meetings, space options may be more limited. Certainly auditoriums and media centers tend to have the most comfortable seating, but what about the cafeteria or the gymnasium? The cafeteria can become more "palatable" if there is an ice cream sundae table or bagel breakfast. The gym bleachers may be used to set a tone for rallying the spirits as staffs prepare to make the final push for some event—a spirit rally with sound information. Off-site locations can provide a faculty with uninterrupted time—free from the distractions of school.

Case in Point

> Desperate for a pick-me-up for the midwinter doldrums, a principal called a restaurant near the school. The owner made a deal for heavy appetizers if the school would have a meeting during the downtime (i.e., 3–4:30 p.m.) when the restaurant would be nearly empty except for school folks attending the meeting. The profits from the faculty drink machine paid the bill. The unexpected can be a welcome diversion from stress and bring professionals back to the goal. No restaurants nearby? Then check the public libraries or parks and recreation centers, which often have conference rooms and auditoriums that are free or charge little to schools. The chairs are often more comfortable than the molded plastic school chairs. When changing sites, be sure to send e-mail reminders and perhaps even make a school-wide announcement.

Create a faculty bulletin board. Take pictures by grades, departments, or teams. Label the pictures with names and content areas, and then post them. Depending on the technology available, the posting may be on the cork bulletin or looping on an in-house TV channel. If the pictures are digital, consider importing the pictures into PowerPoint and labeling them there. Then print out the slides for posting. At the same time, e-mail the slides to faculty members. With access to the slides, faculty members may use them for their reference, such as looking up an unfamiliar or new face to learn a name. If the faculty lounge has a bulletin board, a take on a grade-school activity often called "star of the week" in which faculty and staff members all answer the same questions such as, What is your position at the school? How many years have you worked in education? What did you do before you were a teacher or worked in the school? Where did you go to school? Where is your hometown? What are your pets? Describe your family. Then the sheet along with the staff member's picture could be posted. If teachers know each other's professional practice fairly well, they could post, or write graffiti style, compliments or quotes about the teacher around the picture. A staff member, who could be delegated or who may volunteer, could change the photograph periodically.

These ideas focus on getting to know others in both personal and professional ways. Teachers are mothers, fathers, sons, daughters, *and* educational professionals. They are athletes, travelers, community activists *and* educational professionals. Honoring all roles teachers play in their lives opens communication for similar interests and instructional strengths.

Design Inviting Opportunities for Staff Interactions

Directly linking topics to teachers, students, and school needs by using anecdotes, stories, humor, and multiple sources is one way to create motivating and inviting opportunities. When communication is attractive and interesting, it will result in "greater interest, more cognitive responses, higher message recall, and greater topic recall" (Hallahan, 2000, p. 468). Such motivating interactions may occur at well-planned and engaging faculty meetings, professional development sessions, or more informally.

Teachers are the single most influential school-related factor in student learning as such they deserve to have well-planned and well-executed engaging opportunities.

Teachers on their first day in the classroom are very different from the teachers they will be upon exiting the classroom on the last day of their teaching careers. Ideally, all have grown, improved, shared, innovated, and reflected. However, one-size-fits-all professional development rarely meets the needs of all teachers. An inviting activity to serve different needs, for example, could be school, department, or grade leaders participating in study groups to talk about professional practice rather than looking to the leader for information (Jorgenson & Peal, 2008). Effective professional development opportunities share a common theme in that they build the individual teacher capacity so that high standards are nurtured. Keep in mind the following key ideas as you plan for professional development:

- ❏ Base activities on the needs of teachers in my building or school district.
- ❏ Connect student performance standards with teachers' work.
- ❏ Immerse teachers in experimentation.
- ❏ Provide intensive and sustained support for teachers.
- ❏ Link directly to teachers' work in the classroom.
- ❏ Involve the teachers in concrete training.
- ❏ Increase teachers' content skills by focusing on subject matter.
- ❏ Include structures for collaboration with other teachers.
- ❏ Connect with the overall vision and mission of the school and school district.
- ❏ Commit follow-up support by the administrator or staff member who is implementing the professional development (Adams, 2000; Alliance for Excellent Education, 2005; Supovitz, 2000).

Ideas from the Field

Make the most of new teacher and staff orientation weeks. Whether you are a principal, supervisor, or superintendent, planning the first day back for teachers is an adventure. One principal said, "Just as I like our children to be excited about school, I like my teachers to be excited about the school year." So the month before teachers report for the new school year, they are mailed an agenda for the first week and a letter with a little twist. Written on themed paper, it hints about clothing to wear on their first day back. When the day arrives, the teachers are ready for a surprise, and the school delivers with the auditorium decorated to set the tone for a theme such as *Expedition Excellence* or *Mardi Gras*. How excited teachers may be, or perhaps intrigued, when they get to wear Hawaiian shirts because the school is *Surfing for Higher Waves*. When the teachers arrive to school that morning they are greeted with a lei, have their pictures taken with their team members by a surfboard (pictures are used to make a bulletin board in the main office), and walk onto what appears to be a boardwalk with food to match the theme.

In many school systems, teachers new to the district start work a few days before the rest of their colleagues. The days are often filled with orientation meetings about the school, district, benefits, and policies. Since teacher leaders, such as department chairs, often have extended contracts and are working during this time, create an orientation experience that includes the teacher leaders as an integral part of sharing the culture of the school. *It's Magic* could be a theme in which teacher leaders share some tools for success.

Case in Point

As Halley walked through the office during the new teacher orientation week, she overheard one of her new teachers talking on the telephone to someone who was obviously a new teacher in another school within the district. As Halley entered her office, the new teacher came to her and said, "I am so glad to be here." Smiling, Halley affirmed that she was glad to have him join her staff and asked what prompted him to share the sentiment. The new teacher explained that his fiancée was at another elementary school and for her first day she was given a schedule, keys to her room, and a one-hour orientation to the building that included an introduction of the administrative staff and a movie on bloodborn pathogens. By contrast, Halley's lead team, including administrators and grade-level chairs, had organized a space-themed day called *Blasting Off to a Successful School Year*, where participants got to know people and resources in the school, the instructional objectives, and how each person contributed to the success of the school. The mixture of fun and seriousness to the daylong event made it worthwhile for all.

Support a hospitality committee. Hospitality committees plan staff lunches and get-to-know you interactions. Clear support by the administrator through both financial support and presence communicates that hospitality is a part of the school culture. The hospitality committee may organize potluck luncheons during various lunch periods—food definitely brings people together.

Generate staff spirit. All schools have something about which they are proud. It may be having the best cafeteria food in the district or a strong athletic program. For many schools, it is making achievement gains. Thunder sticks, bumper stickers, etc. can be donated that can make events a bit more fun.

Case in Point

For most of the year, a refrain heard in the school was "Let's get in the green zone." Teachers and students had been motivated all year to be in the green zone (area where success was likely) as opposed to red (area of significant concern) and yellow (area where extra work was needed). Initiatives to help students succeed were in place. As mandatory standardized testing geared up in the school, a green T-shirt designed by the students that said "R U N the Zone?" was printed. The T-shirts were available for $5. If one read the shirt as a text message, it asked "Are you in the zone?" Students and teachers bought them up, bringing a lift to the grueling month-long testing period.

Host a school scavenger hunt. Faculties can be competitive. Often staff meetings have a focus, so actively engage teachers in looking for best practices or items related to the meeting's focus. For example, if the meeting is about 21st-century learning practices, e-mail a scavenger hunt sheet the week before a staff meeting so teachers can note when they see good practices. If school safety is the focus, consider starting the staff meeting off with a 10-minute scavenger hunt around the building to identify particular issues, then discuss. For a purely fun, morale-boosting scavenger hunt, read the following Author's Tale.

> **Author's Tale**
> **A Just-for-Fun Morale Boost**
>
> For teacher appreciation week, a different theme was identified for each day of the week. The first day on the calendar was: Do rams lay eggs? (The school's mascot is a ram). The secretaries hid eggs with donated prizes and gift cards around the school. At the faculty meeting that afternoon, the teachers found out their school's mascot did lay eggs. They went on an egg hunt around the building (egg hunting participation was optional). I got on the intercom and announced that Mrs. Smith just found a $10 gift certificate to the teacher's store. The teachers were excited, it was fun to watch, and the hunt was a welcome stress reliever. [Administrators, be aware as sometimes a hallway referee is needed as teachers can get competitive, and school rules still apply—there should be no running in the halls!] The teachers loved this event—an example of what Stephen Covey, author and inspirational speaker, calls a win-win situation.
>
> After a few years of doing a schoolwide scavenger hunt using plastic eggs, I was thinking about doing something different. However, after overhearing a teacher's conversation about how they look forward to it every year and my secretary telling me that there was no way I was changing, I smiled as I realized that we had what is now a school tradition on the first Monday of teacher appreciation week.
>
> —Angie Seiders

Productive Messages and Feedback

Leadership styles often predispose leaders to certain ways of sharing material. Bolman and Deal (1997) talk about frames of leadership that influence the way information is packaged for communication. The *structural frame* is "just the facts, ma'am," the *political frame* concerns persuasive information, the *symbolic frame* often packages material in a story, and the *human relations frame* focuses on the needs of people as well as information. Regardless of the packaging, leaders need to communicate their commitments through words and actions with a clear guiding purpose (Kouzes & Posner, 2002; Smith, 2001). Effective leaders tailor their messages to reach their followers and workers.

A survey asked 47 teachers how often they discussed a series of education-related issues with their school's two principals. The choices were: weekly, 1 to 2 times a month, 1 to 2 times a semester, rarely, and no response. On a weekly basis, principals and teachers conversed about rules (22%) comfort (17%), action plans (14%), school improvement, academic goals, social goals (8% each), results (6%), and quality, curriculum issues, vision, and feedback (3% each) (Ärlestig, 2007). A red flag may be raising right about now, as instruction, assessment, and collaboration are noticeably absent from the weekly discussions. Teachers (61%) reported that instruction was rarely discussed; grades were focused upon on a semester basis (75%), and teamwork was rarely mentioned (47%) (Ärlestig). In the same study, teachers said that they liked principals to communicate positive results and support for the teachers. Communication through e-mail, face-to-face interactions, telephones, and so forth maintains a focus on key issues for educators and leadership. Leaders are inextricably dependent upon their ability to communicate with stakeholders. Their communication competence determines their effectiveness.

Use Effective Techniques

Leader-member relations, rapport management, and *communicator competence* are just a few of the terms used by researchers in the communication and leadership fields to discuss effective communication techniques. Studies have found a link between perceived leader communication competence and employee job satisfaction (see for example, Lewis, 2006; Madlock, 2008; Sharbrough, Simmons, & Cantrill, 2006). The words that a leader chooses and how those words are ordered and delivered affect how the message is communicated (Madlock, 2008; Sias, 2005). A trio of researchers classified leaders' communication styles into four categories (see Figure 3.2). Depending on the situation, a particular style may be more appropriate. Researchers have found that leaders often have a preference for one of the styles (Campbell, White, & Johnson, 2003). However, leaders who are adept at selecting the appropriate way to share information with others achieve higher results (Hart & Quinn, 1993). The accurate transmission of the message is facilitated by the use of multiple modes of communication (Barkhi, Varghese, & Pirkul, 11999) and the use of different message styles.

| Figure 3.2. Communication with Purpose |||
Category	Purpose	Case in Point Example
Informational	Provides facts	The predictor test in social studies will be given next Tuesday.
Relational	Builds trust	Let me know how your students do on Tuesday's social studies predictor test.
Instructional	Directs action	Once you score the social studies predictor test, examine items that had a high percent of students missing them and determine an appropriate response such as reteaching, reviewing, teaching students a test-taking skill.
Transformational	Starts change	What do you plan to do with the results of the social studies predictor test after you administer and score it?

Note: The first and second columns are based on the work of Campbell, K. S., White, C. D., & Johnson, D. E.(2003). Leader-member relations as a function of rapport management. The *Journal of Business Communication*, 40(3),170–195.Retrieved on April 8, 2008, from http://find.galegroup.com.proxy.wm.edu/itx/start.do?prodId=EAIM

An instructional leader can set the tone for the action that is to come by the use of motivational language. Mayfield and Mayfield (2006) defined three forms of motivational language: direction-giving (i.e., clarification of goals); empathetic (i.e., emotional understanding of followers' situation); and meaning-making (i.e., stories, metaphors). A school's strongest cheerleader should be the school's principal; likewise the department's advocate would be the department chair. Self-efficacy theory indicates that the degree to which a teacher believes that she or he can make a difference is tied to the support the teacher receives and the motivation provided (Tschannen-Moran & Hoy, 2001). A study found that the use of motivational language was a positive indicator of the leader's communication competence, effectiveness, and communication satisfaction as perceived by employees (Sharbrough et al., 2006). In another study of professionals, researchers found that full-time workers of leaders who used motivating language were more satisfied with their jobs and had higher levels of performance than counterparts with less motivating leaders (Mayfield & Mayfield, 2006). Simply put, how you say something matters.

Ideas from the Field

Comment on what is right and going well. Deliberate communication actions can yield a multitude of benefits. For this field idea, the purpose is to make a concerted effort to have positive dialogue. All too often when "things" are going well, general group feedback is given. For example, at a science department meeting following the school fair, the department chair may acknowledge how all the hard work resulted in a successful event. However, this is a general statement aimed at everyone. Yet, even the most humble among us appreciates knowing that his or her efforts were noticed. Calling out specific contributions and saying "Good job for keeping students engaged while they waited for the judges, Mr. Hill," communicates a valuing of that person's contributions. Likewise, never underestimate the power of a couple of quickly jotted lines on a thank-you card that acknowledge a specific contribution or action. And if they do not keep them, encourage them to do so. Provide teachers with "Good Notes" folders where they can keep positive messages from fellow teachers, administrators, students, and parents. These notes are often reread on tough days and even kept for years!

Pull people back together. Professionals have differing opinions on instructional approaches, resources, top issues, and a host of other topics. Collegial discussions are beneficial for identifying issues, defining issues, and focusing efforts. These discussions can become intense and even heated. Before letting folks leave the table, seek to have everyone getting on the same page—one turned to the interests of students.

Have "difficult" conversations in person. Technology has made communication more immediate yet at times more remote. Addressing a concern in e-mail can exacerbate a situation as there is no face-to-face interaction and relying solely on words without the benefit of nonverbal communication can result in a very different message being received. The e-mail is most likely to be viewed as one-way communication, rather than a conversation in which a difficult issue needs to be discussed and resolved. If an issue needs to be addressed, have the conversation with the teacher one-to-one and face-to-face.

Send e-mails that convey your intent. Effective e-mails have subject lines that give the receiver a "heads up" on the content of the e-mail, a message that is clear, and a signature line that clearly identifies the sender as not all e-mail addresses are easily discerned. These tips may sound like common sense, but they can ensure that your message is received and understood as you intend:

- Turn on the spell check feature. There is no reason to have misspellings that will distract the reader or worse yet make the sender want to send a follow-up "corrected" version.
- Reread the message before hitting "Send" to ensure that the message is clear.
- Consider the length of the message. If a message requires scrolling the screen image, it may be better to attach the item. Or, the initial message could be written with a "see below" so that the reader gets the main body text without the interruption of a longer object. For example, when sending a teacher a draft of the department's grading policy, write the entire message and reference the policy that is either attached or appears at the end of the e-mail.
- Use "Reply All" judiciously. If the response needs to go to only one individual, there is no need to fill up everyone else's e-mail box.
- Send e-mails in a timely manner that allows for time sensitive responses to be given or action taken.

Case in Point

A first-year teacher received an e-mail from her principal before Thanksgiving break telling her that he wanted to talk to her after the holiday about a call from a parent he had received. The e-mail was sent near the end of the school day, and the principal was gone when the teacher went to look for him. For the young teacher, the principal's e-mail was akin to being called to the principal's office. She wondered, "What have I done wrong?" Her colleagues saw that she was upset before the holiday, and she was still upset after the long weekend. When the principal saw her during her planning period on Monday, he told that he wanted to share with her the compliment he had received about her in person. The e-mail did not accurately convey the intent and resulted in a stressful holiday weekend.

Speak the language. Many years ago, a school system had a staff development offering called "It Takes Two to Tango." Session activities were aimed at increasing awareness and effectiveness of how one communicates. The facilitator demonstrated how different people interpret the same message differently. The key is to listen to how someone "packages" a message. People who just give the facts tend to prefer receiving succinct responses; whereas, individuals who tell stories in order to illustrate a point, appreciate more narrative responses.

Support communication. Use minutes and agendas to maintain the communication lines. Since school leaders can not be in all places at all times or realistically attend every meeting that occurs in the school, "meeting minute monitoring" is a good communication practice. Quickly reviewing meeting minutes provides a validation that what needs to occur is happening or may highlight an issue that needs addressing. This monitoring keeps the focus on progress and accomplishments on the table. Feedback often can be sent back via e-mail or written on the hardcopy to be placed in the teacher's box. Agendas let folks know what is going to occur. An agenda that has a section for "course of action" could provide a forum for noting upcoming reports and offer a place where employees know that they will have to address items relevant to their job. Well constructed agendas let folks know what is ahead, provide an opportunity for revision and reflection, and provides meeting participants a voice.

Case in Point

A communication forum is a school's blog, copier room, or faculty lounge. For the low-tech version, have someone create a bulletin board complete with post-it notes where faculty members can write a question such as "What have you done when the kids keep throwing paper balls, but you can not identify the culprits?" Teachers can use the post-it notes to respond with ideas. This is an anonymous way for someone to get some insight. Likewise a school or department blog or electronic bulletin board is another means to facilitate the exchange of information. Guidelines such as "no student names, no negative remarks, etc." should be given.

Get back to people. Simple business 101, let people know you got their message, whether they are the superintendent, parent, teachers, or someone else. If the leader's practice is respond to e-mails and telephone messages within 24 hours, then tell teachers this is the expectation. Even a response that indicates that a follow up communication is needed is better than no response. Likewise, remember to give vacation notices—handy for when someone cannot be reached for a period of time.

Avoid Pitfalls That Undermine Your Intent

Ever been in one of the following situations? Someone asks for your opinion and then starts talking. A question is posed and then the speaker answers the question immediately. The person with whom you are talking does not seem to be listening. Opened an e-mail with a few typos only to get another e-mail apologizing for the typos? With all the folks you need to communicate with, being a teacher leader or school administrator is tough. Communication missteps may sometimes occur and being aware of pitfalls makes them easier to avoid. Figure 3.3 identifies three common potential pitfalls and ways to avoid them.

Ideas from the Field

Stay focused. Maintaining a clear mind during difficult situations is beneficial to being able to navigate the situation. If someone is agitated, angry, or even yelling, go to a calm place in your mind and respond in an even tone. First address safety concerns (e.g., an adult punching furniture). If there are no safety concerns, then discern what the issue is and address it. There are times when as school leaders we know that a difficult conversation is going to occur and likely the other party involved is going to get upset. Having a couple of key points that must be conveyed

\	Figure 3.3. Strategies to Overcome Potential Communication Pitfalls	
Potential Pitfalls	**Research**	**Strategy**
Commands—When information must be given quickly	There are two types commands: *alpha commands* consisting of a single idea or verb, are simple and direct, and *beta commands* consisting of several action verbs take more time to process as multiple directions or ideas are provided (Matheson & Schriver, 2005).	Allowing a 3- to 5-second response time between commands increases the likelihood that the request will be accurately processed and followed.
Wait time—When a question is posed and imaginary crickets can be heard in the silence	Wait time is beneficial as listeners can process the inquiry and formulate a response (Rowe, 1972). There are two kinds of wait time: wait time 1 is the silence right after the question is posed, and wait time 2 is the pause after the speaker responds before the next speaker. Both are useful as wait time 2 often generates more involvement, understanding, and application.	Count slowly to three.
Communication Mode—When to talk in person and when to use text messaging and other electronic means	The researchers measured decision quality, quality of the information exchanged, and group processing measures including time, efficiency, and perceived frustration on problem solving. They found that employees and leaders were more forthcoming when communicating face-to-face compared with online. Further individuals in the computer group were more likely to get frustrated than counterparts communicating in person (Barkhi, Varghese, & Pirkul, 1999).	Consider and anticipate how much interaction will be necessary to address the topic. Then select an appropriate communication mode.

is a means to ensuring that the conversation is not derailed. Eliminating distractions to focus on the concern is your strategy.

Case in Point

Miranda always wanted to be a teacher, and it is a core facet of her identity. Miranda was a good teacher—maybe even great, but now she is off her game. Everyone in the school knows that her sister is receiving hospice care, her mother-in-law recently moved in, and she is essentially raising two kids on her own as her husband travels on business. Miranda's resilience has protected her students and her through difficult life transitions, but now cracks are being seen and her students are beginning to show signs of her stress. Her assistant principal knows that this conversation will not be easy as Miranda is likely to feel blindsided or even attacked.

As he meets with Miranda, the assistant principal holds an index card with a couple of key talking points with examples. Miranda is upset, even angry that her performance is called into question. Tears flow as she begins to acknowledge the impact her personal life is having on her students. As the conversation meanders, the card helps the assistant principal return to the school issues while providing sympathy and support.

Let folks know if you are planning to check behind them. Teacher leaders and administrative leaders often delegate tasks. For most tasks, once delegated, the receiving person has total ownership of the duty and provides updates to the leader. However, there are those tasks that a leader must watch closely, regardless of how well the assigned person is doing. For example, a principal may delegate the generation of the annual yearly progress (AYP) updates, but, given the nature of the report, requires that each one cross his or her desk prior to taking further action. Let the delegated individual know ahead that these will be checked, because of the nature of the task rather than because of a lack of confidence in the person's abilities.

Define who "they" are. The pronoun "they" often gets loosely used. If the technology specialist voices a complaint by saying, "They are always late to the schoolwide technology mini-in-services." Defining "they" may be 5 out of 100 staff members, so it would not be appropriate to remind everyone to be on time. The majority who are on time will likely will be annoyed that instead of addressing the people that everyone knows are always late, the principal's message used a passive-aggressive approach. Likewise, a teacher leader commenting on a proposed initiative may say that "They would not like it." Ask who constitutes "they." As in the hypothetical comment above, "they" might actually be one person stuck in the mud, rather resistant to change, a difficult teacher. Simply put, focus efforts on the person(s), not a generic "they." A good leader is also often good at asking questions—especially those that help staff arrive at an answer.

Don't applaud mediocrity. An occupational hazard of educators is constantly trying to see the good. It may sound like common sense, but do not give positive feedback for incompetence. Leadership should be actively working to scaffold learning experiences for the professional whose performance is ineffective so that he or she can provide competent and quality teaching for students.

Use the tone of the voice to convey emotion. The speaker's voice will convey urgency, calm, or a host other emotions, so often it is not necessary to articulate what one is feeling By modulating the tone of your voice, listeners know to focus on what is to be done as opposed responding to an emotion. For example using the right tone of voice might be a leader saying calmly in response to a tornado siren, "Everyone will walk to the basement level and remain quietly until the tornado warning is over."

Take time to compose yourself. While there are some situations that require immediate reaction, most situations can simmer. Common sense suggests that having conversations when we are upset is not good. So consider the following activities that can create composure time: Write a statement, schedule a meeting, invite someone else to join you, suggest an alternate venue, or ask the person for additional information.

Show What Is Valued

How do we communicate the fundamental value of staff, students, and our schools? Being knowledgeable about a teacher's instructional situation and students demonstrates an investment in learning. One teacher compared her current principal to past principals. "I've had principals who've never been in a room unless there's some crisis, and they don't have a clue as to what is going on. He's [principal] in here . . . He knows my kids, he knows my teaching style. It makes a huge difference" (Paglin, 2000, p. 2).

Another way of communicating value is showing we care about the person. A teacher tells of a principal who affirmed her value as a teacher when she had a rough morning getting to work by asking her what he could do to help; he did not ask questions about why the teacher was off her game, and his supportive actions set a positive tone (Harris, 2004). Caring actions may be a kind word, an inquiry following up on previously shared information, such as asking how a teacher's son is doing if the teacher had taken off a few days due to her child breaking his ankle.

Consider the following findings from research studies that demonstrate the value of showing what is valued in an organization:

- A study found that when leaders clearly articulated the vision for an organization and valued employee input, employees had more expectations for success. Furthermore, the quality of the information given is vital to gaining the support of staff (Lewis, 2006).
- In another study of communication between supervisors and subordinates, the researcher found that more than half of the differences in perceived relationship quality as reported by the subordinates could be accounted by the amount and quality of the information shared by supervisors (Sias, 2005).
- A study of principal leadership at outstanding schools in New South Wales (Australia) found that common characteristics of the principals in the study included that they (1) communicated the value of students and staff to the students and staff and (2) positively promote the school to stakeholders (Dinham, 2005).

Ideas from the Field

Show passion. What is valued should not be a secret or even a multiple choice question. If the bottom line focus is "what is good for kids" then everyone who spends even two minutes in the building should know that is what the leadership stresses. Be willing to work beside your teachers to help and support. Recognize the passion of others. For example, if good instruction is a component of a teacher's passion, then talk about it, observe it, reflect upon it, and create situations where new teachers and struggling teachers can see good models in action.

Plan for sharing what is valued. Faculty and department meetings often are professional development opportunities rather than checking off agenda items. Survey teachers about what they would like to have as miniprofessional developments, then let folks know that the session reflects the findings from the survey. The survey has the added benefit of being a valuable tool to identify different offerings for teachers as veteran, midcareer, and novice teachers very rarely have the same professional growth needs. Plan and prepare for periodic intense focus on the values of the school or department using the different offerings. If there are to be 10 miniprofessional development opportunities, do the long-range planning and tell folks what to expect. Tell them what your expectations are for their participation.

Be open to building understanding. What may be small, trivial, and insignificant to some may have farther reaching implications. For example, some people have "Hi" issues. They get upset because someone didn't say "Hi" in the morning or asked them how they were doing. So if they don't say hello every morning, just keep smiling and saying good morning and perhaps ask them "How is everything?" After all, teachers do this to build relationships with students, why not each other? If there is a concern about interactions, address the issue, and encourage positive action.

Case in Point

There is a story about the man on the train with his three children who were acting up on the train-yelling, screaming, and running around. The other passengers were watching. Finally, after the kids acted up for a long period of time, someone asked "Can't you control your kids?" The father looked and said, "I am so sorry, their mother died this morning." The point of the story is that one never knows what is going on in someone's personal life.

Recap

- Effective communication enhances employee job satisfaction and performance.
- Communication makes people feel a part of a school, committee, or department.
- The way in which a message is delivered matters.
- Relationships respond to the quality of the communication between the people involved in them.
- Teachers want clear, specific, and individual feedback.

Reflection Moment

Take 3 to 8 minutes to think about the following questions.

- How well do I create welcoming situations in which staff members can communicate about educational issues?
- Looking at Figure 3.2, which style do I use most often? Which one do I prefer to hear when someone is communicating with me?
- Which one of the *Ideas from the Field* could I try this week? Use in the future?

4

Team Sense: Choose Them Wisely, Use Them Wisely, or Lose Them Completely

Team sense is simply all the knowledge that leaders have about their faculties. There are the basics such as amount of years of teaching experience and current teaching assignment. Yet, school leaders with highly developed team sense know individual teachers' strengths and potential areas for professional growth. They know intuitively or through observation when to push and when to hold back. They even know bits and pieces about their teachers' lives outside of the schoolhouse doors which further builds the connection between them. Team sense enables leaders to get the faculty to function better together than an individual could do alone.

The sub-title of the chapter refers to the need to invest in teachers. Teachers are both the major resource and major expenditure in schools. When people feel valued, their job satisfaction is high. School system budgets typically allocate 85% of the available funds towards personnel and benefits such as insurance premiums and retirement contributions.

Figure 4.1

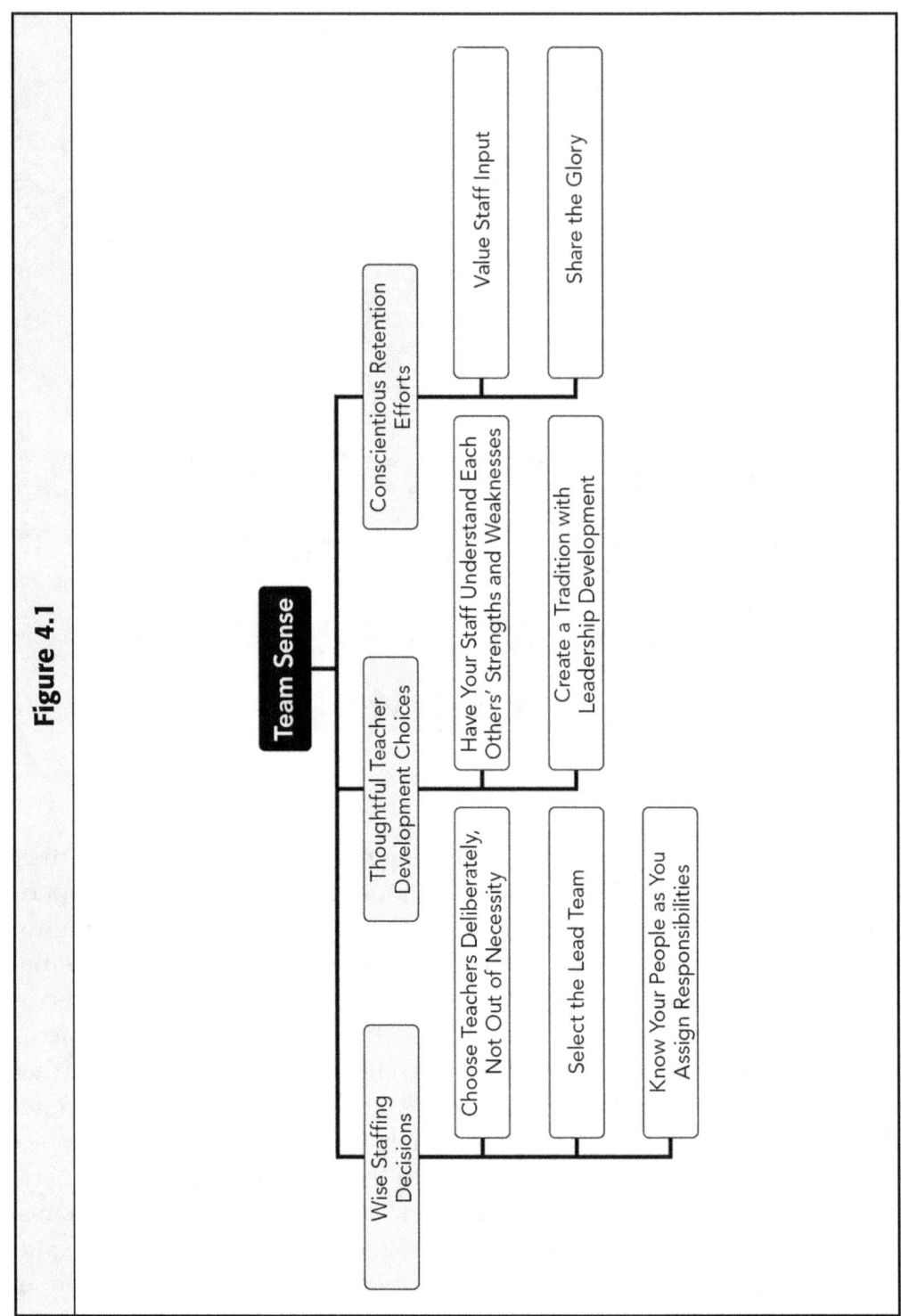

Such a lion's portion of funds represents a substantial investment in teachers. Yet, this investment for many is passive, like buying a savings bond, placing it in a safety deposit box, and waiting for it to mature as opposed to investing in a high-yield account, monitoring performance, and making necessary adjustments to enhance performance. Just as one loses money if a savings bond is lost, the cost of teacher turnover is high. One study estimated that filling a teaching position is valued at 25% to 33% of the teacher's salary by the time recruitment, administrative, and training costs were calculated (Texas Center for Educational Research, 2002). Another article indicated that in the United States teacher transfers to other schools and new teacher hiring costs 4.9 billon dollars a year (Alliance for Excellent Education, 2005).

Teachers are increasingly in demand as student enrollment rises, reductions in class size are mandated, and the current teacher workforce nears retirement. Thus, by the 2015–2016 school year, K–12 enrollment in public and private schools is expected to reach 57.6 million students (Snyder, Dillow, & Hoffman, 2007). Yet, teachers are leaving the profession and retiring faster than certified new hires can be secured. Approximately 50% of teachers who entered the teaching profession left within five years (Ingersoll, 2001). Compounding this problem is that 39% of newly certified teachers decide not to teach (Darling-Hammond, 2000; Edwards, 2000). Nearly 64% of teachers who leave the profession are employed by private businesses, 18.8% work for the government, and 11.9% are self-employed (Pigge & Marso, 1996). A related issue to the shortage is the mismatch of where teachers are located and where the need exists for certain subject matter or grade-level endorsements. Clearly, we need to do a better job of retaining educators.

Investing in teachers is about words and actions. This chapter focuses on the investment in human resources—an investment we call "team sense." Figure 4.1 provides an overview of the chapter. In the same way, teachers are asked to monitor their investment in students, instructional leaders must monitor their investment in teachers.

Wise Staffing Decisions

Personnel decisions can seem to fly into school offices like snowballs—scarcely is one decision made when another need comes flying at administrators. Central office may assign or reassign personnel. Principals recommend the hiring of new teachers. Staff members may resign or ask for transfers. This chapter focuses on the decisions that are often within an instructional leader's domain of influence.

A school system's human resources department typically leads recruitment efforts, and the final selection is the school leader's decision. It is the impression left by the school-based personnel that weighs heavily in an applicant's decision to sign a contract. In one study, 94% of teachers surveyed said strong and supportive school leadership was a major factor in their decision to work in a school (Hirsch, 2006). In addition to interviewing applicants who are new to the school, instructional leaders can recruit from within, identifying promising para-educators to pursue licensure (Genzuk, 1997) and encouraging good and effective substitutes to apply for positions open in their building. A well-run school with colleagues who care about each other and share common goals is a powerful incentive (Inman & Marlow, 2004). Be part of the reason that someone says "yes" to teaching in your building.

Choose Teachers Deliberately, Not Out of Necessity

Teacher hiring needs to be efficient and targeted. Select teachers based on the strengths they offer. Consider their value-added potential. When putting together teams and grade levels, think about how teachers' strengths will complement one another. Selection and teacher recruitment are interdependent, so let the school or district recruiting personnel know of anticipated hiring needs as well as desired qualifications of the person who would fit those needs (Wise, Darling-Hammond, & Berry, 1987).

Teacher leader involvement in the selection of new staff members is beneficial. A survey of more than four thousand licensed Alabama educators found that 95.8% of respondents considered opportunities to participate in school decision-making processes (e.g., hiring, budgets) as an important nonfinancial incentive to teach in hard-to-staff schools (Hirsh, 2006). Further, involving teacher leaders, "enhances the validity of the process by providing greater insight into candidates' subject matter competence," according to researchers conducting case studies on teacher selection (Wise et al., 1987, p. viii). Teacher leaders and administrators can work together "to create a learning environment that would attract a solid professional corps of teachers" (Quinn, 2005, p. 225). In this way, the school sells itself to prospective teachers.

Ideas from the Field

Involve current teachers in the interview for their next colleague. There are multiple benefits to including teachers on the interview team. First and foremost is their expertise in knowing what works within the content or grade level. Imagine interviewing for a band director-teacher position, but the interviewer is musically illiterate. Or more commonly, the interviewer has knowledge of pedagogy, but not of the specific subject matter, so the interviewer is at a disadvantage in assessing the applicant's content knowledge. Another benefit is getting the current staff invested in the prospective new hire. While confidentiality binds the tongues of teachers participating in the interview, preventing them from telling their colleagues about interviewees, the fact of their presence on the interview panel communicates that staff had input into who was selected to join the school. Finally, having a teacher on the interview panel sends a message to the applicant that teachers are valued. The applicant may also begin to identify with that teacher and provide additional details about skills, issues, or strategies related to the content area as the applicant knows there is a knowledgeable, content-area person in the room who can relate to the answer.

Share what the expectations are for faculty members at the school and in the department. Some expectations are commonsense such as be on time, whereas others are unique. Therefore, focus on what is different about a school's expectations. For example, tell applicants what the department does to help children be successful. A prospective new teacher may be energized by the teaching initiatives or, on the other hand, realize that this is not the place for her—either way, the school benefits. Sharing expectations is powerful too when the instructional leader is new to the school or recently assigned to lead a grade level. In this case, the expectations are part of the information shared with staff so they know what is coming. Of course, just like with our students, it is vital that expectations have meaning and follow-through rather than being merely introductory statements.

Make the best of necessity situations—a little goodwill can go a long way. There are times when staff members are not the ideal fit for the school because of involuntary transfers, a small applicant pool, or perhaps times have changed but the staff member has not. Extend a welcome to the new staff member. Be positive and proactive with targeted praise and sharing of your vision. Also be vigilant; address concerns early and specifically.

Case in Point

A principal was in a situation in which several teachers were transferring into her school from other schools in the school system. A few of the teachers were mandatory transfers as a school closed in the district. To make all intra-district transfer staff members feel welcome, this leader bought several roses at the grocery store and had a tag attached to each one to welcome the teachers transferring into the building. The roses were then delivered by the secretary to the school office where the teachers were finishing out the school year. Through the school system grapevine, the principal heard that teachers were ecstatic when they received their roses.

Select The Lead Team

Often, a principal is assigned to a school in which the lead team (see gray box Chapter 2 for definition) is already in place. However, if you are a leader who is offered the opportunity to build the lead team or department, consider this one of the most important job responsibilities as these professionals are an extension of you. Researchers in a study on school violence recommended that principals have greater input in selecting their administrative teams as cohesiveness of actions of the team is important; further, students in the schools experiencing difficulty identified a lack of cohesiveness among the actions of their schools' leadership (Wood & Huffman, 1999). Having a reliable core team allows the leader of the team to designate specific responsibilities for each member and cultivate a culture of shared leadership. Finding the right people may be the result of outside hires, promotions, or rewriting job descriptions, and developing the lead team requires an investment of time as members learn or adapt to their new roles and the faculty adjusts to them (Votey,

2002). A viable lead team provides support for its members, school initiatives, faculty, staff members, and students.

Ideas from the Field

Advocate on behalf of the school or your department to the decision makers for permission to recommend replacements or fill new slots. If the "higher ups" determine that the best interest of the school system would be to promote or transfer a member of your team, do not sit and wait to see who they will give you to fill the slot. Request to have input into who will fill the slot because it is you who has the best interests of the school or department in mind.

Consider the balance of other members of the lead team so that strengths and weaknesses complement and compensate for one another. Look for positive attitude, loyalty, commitment to students, and a strong work ethic. Some skills can be developed within an established team, but personal characteristics as these are prerequisites in selecting new members.

Check the references and call colleagues. Some administrators maintain that checking references is a waste of time because references are not always forthcoming or because references are picked by the applicant. Check the references anyway for your short list of candidates. References often are more candid on the telephone than they are in letters of recommendation. If the applicant is within the school district or a system where you have colleagues, call them to ask about the applicant's work ethic and how they perceive the professional. Checking references can validate your opinion that was formed during a review of the application and during the interview. The practice of checking references can also be priceless if you find out that the applicant nearly put one over on you by giving the impression that his or her experiences were more extensive or positive than a reference will confirm.

Case in Point

A simple reference check yielded unexpected information. The applicant had a strong resume showing increasing responsibilities over the last 7 years—from teacher to assistant principal in two local school systems. The applicant had applied for a position as a principal in yet another school system. Since each move in a sense was a promotion and opportunities for administrators in the area could be sparse, the changing school districts was not a red flag as it would have been if a teacher was moving every 2 to 3 years. The interview was very strong, so before making a job offer, the references were checked. A call to the current supervisor (who had written a rather benign reference letter) took an unexpected turn when the question was asked, "Is there anything else about this applicant's work that you would like to share?" At that point, the applicant's current supervisor acknowledged that the applicant could work a room and make a good first impression, but the second impression left much to be desired as the applicant did not work well with staff and seemingly avoided instructional issues.

Know Your People As You Assign Responsibilities

Consider what is in the best interest of the school as well as the professional when deciding teaching assignments and extra duties. Effective leaders are in the field; they know how their teachers instruct and what the teachers' styles are (Paglin, 2000). Leaders take care in how staff is selected and assigned—even if it means that a decision made in the best interest of the school may be unpopular (Dinham, 2005). They are watching, participating, and providing feedback.

Ideas from the Field

Demonstrate professional courtesy. Rather than simply telling a teacher to take on a teaching assignment or duties, meet with him or her first and explain why you made the decision and believe it to be in the best interest of the students or school. This helps to create an environment where the stronger teachers understand why they need to support struggling teachers or make a difference for students in a critical year (e.g., testing year, transition to or from school levels).

Case in Point

Some teachers may be reluctant to move to a high stakes testing and low test score situation. In an elementary school, the grade-level chair was consulted by her principal about the need for an effective teacher to move to a challenging situation. The principal thought that the grade-level chair was the appropriate choice. When the principal explained the need and asked the teacher, "Who do we move?" she responded, "Me."

Balance the needs of the school or department with what is in the best interests of the professional. Most job descriptions include a catch-all statement about "other duties as assigned." Be particularly careful not to overload the same people, but consider other teachers who have potential, but they may not have fully demonstrated yet. The Pareto Principle says 20% of the people do 80% of the work. Overloading some and not developing others can adversely affect relationships in the school when stress and frustration levels build as they do around critical times of the school year. By judiciously managing personnel as a resource, the instructional leader can help balance the stress load that extra duties (even paid ones) bring.

Case in Point

The principal and administrative team kept coming up with Joe's name for a particular duty, but Joe was already heavily committed elsewhere. No one else seemed to fit the bill and blanks were being drawn. The principal solicited Joe's input by telling him about the opportunity and how the principal knew that if Joe took it on, he would make it his own and do a fantastic job. He told Joe that he did not want to add another hat to Joe's hat rack and asked him who else could do the duty. Joe gave his principal some teachers' names with a brief assessment of what each individual would offer. Of the colleagues he mentioned, he really thought that, Xian would do an outstanding job. Sometimes teachers are aware of colleagues' expertise or ambitions that have not yet been recognized by administration.

Thoughtful Teacher Development Choices

Induction, staff development, and professional development all have the teacher as the focus. How much influence does an instructional leader have over teacher development? The answer is, it depends.

Often induction programs for new teachers are managed by school systems; however, there are ways a leader can maximize the induction process in the building. For example, an administrator may be able to end the "trial by fire" by assigning first-year teachers to positions where they are likely to succeed (Jorissen, 2002); supporting mentoring programs (Darling-Hammond & Berry, n.d.; Inman & Marlow, 2004; Wald, 1998), and providing common planning time for new teachers with experienced teachers in the same grade or content area (Quinn, 2005). A department chair can meet with mentors and support them as they work with new teachers. A teacher leader may visit the classroom of a teacher who is experienced, but new to the building, to answer any questions about how things are done at the school.

Nearly every professional from attorney to teacher has a requirement for continuing education. A school's staff development takes a variety of forms from top-down mandated workshops to professional learning community-initiated activities. Study after educational study has supported the value of professional development for teachers as it relates to student learning and achievement (see for example, Camphire, 2001; Cross & Regden, 2002; Wenglinsky, 2002). As a leader, closely tailoring professional development offerings to teachers' needs is invaluable. As Australian educational researcher John Hattie (2003) said, "It is what teachers know, do, and care about that is very powerful in the learning equation" (p. 2).

Teaching as a career is different from other careers. Novice teachers on the first day of school have the same responsibilities as teachers with many more years of experience. Consider how leaders can support the development of teachers whose aspiration is to be a contributing professional, great teacher, or administrator while they are in the classroom.

Have Your Staff Understand Each Others' Strengths And Weaknesses

Everyone has team experience: some positive and some negative; some in sports and others in school or life. Whether a team is football, grade level, or school improvement there is always a main goal that is supported by plays, initiatives, strategies, and people. Peyton Manning, quarterback for the Indianapolis Colts, was named the 2007 No. 1 National Football League player by *Sports Illustrated* in an article in which he was described as "an ebullient leader and master tactician," (King, 2007, p. 75). Manning knows that the results credited to his leadership are due to teamwork. He says that he does not want his teammates to be awestruck; rather he wants them to work as equals. To that end, he studies the game tapes, asks for input, and knows his players and the opponent's players' tendencies. The NFL's No. 1 player is like many of the highly effective teachers and leaders in today's schools who know their learners' and their coworkers' strengths and needs well and who work hard to support the success of their students and schools.

A school staff is a team, simply put, focused on what is good for kids. As leaders of schools, departments, or fellow teachers, you know the gifts, talents, and areas for improvement of your staffs. Providing forums (e.g., electronic discussion boards, time at the beginning of meetings) for your teachers to interact so they, too, better understand their coworkers strengths and needs is valuable in promoting team sense. Offering professional development opportunities that are relevant to teachers' needs is essential (Jorissen, 2002; Gersten, Keating, Yovanaf, & Harniss, 2001; Otto & Arnold, 2001).

Retain early career teachers by cultivating and supporting them through systematic, intensive, and targeted staff development (Billingsley, 2004). Work to create structures that encourage collegiality such as opportunities for collaboration (Inman & Marlow, 2004; Jorissen, 2002; Wald, 1998) and peer support groups (Whitworth, 2000). Through these interactions, staff members become connected and invested in each other. These steps can be the beginning of a professional learning community and effective professional development that can "engage the hearts and heads of educators in order to keep teachers engaged in active learning," (Peery, 2004, p. 15).

Ideas from the Field

Plan professional developments around staff strengths and weaknesses. Differentiate staff developments. It only stands to reason that whereas many teachers may share a common weakness, not all of them do. Use teachers who have strengths and expertise in a particular area to deliver the professional development for their colleagues because this delivery model can be exceptionally powerful as teacher-to-teacher dialogue ensues. Offer multiple professional developments during the same time frame so teachers can choose. Remember, a professional development that addresses teachers at too low or high a level is just as worthless as a session that does not relate to what the teacher is teaching. Also, be mindful that teachers who are leading the staff development also need opportunities to grow and renew. So ensure that they have opportunities for staff development that align to their skills and need for complexity. Indeed one-size-rarely-fits-all when it comes to professional development.

Encourage others to share what they know. When faculty members request school funds or a professional development day to attend a professional conference or workshop, let them know that you'd like them to share what they learned with others in a grade, department, or faculty meeting, thereby helping to build a culture of professional learning.

Build awareness as interpersonal issues arise. Think about a school staff as a family—folks do not always get along. Ignoring the issue will not make it go away. Sometimes the administrator needs to take the role of the mediator, helping teachers realize the good in their colleagues. For example, a team of four teachers may be frustrated and dysfunctional because they do not understand each other's strengths and weaknesses. It may be that one member of the team is highly task-oriented with a "get it done" approach, and another team member is more visionary with ideas that seem to "float around for a while." These two team members may be in conflict and resent each other, which causes stress for the other two team members. When we learn how each other operates, we can understand one another and build from strength instead of resenting what frustrates us.

Recognize potential and develop it within teachers. Schools are getting better, but there is still a fair amount of isolation among teachers. For example, you might tell a teacher that she differentiates instruction for her high ability and gifted learners exceptionally well. This is news to her because she assumed that everyone did what she does. Providing opportunities for a teacher to make an impact outside of her classroom can develop leadership potential. A small step could be as simple as asking that teacher if she would be willing to share her professional practice with a struggling colleague, then have that colleague contact the teacher. A larger step may be recommending a teacher for additional paid opportunities that provide exposure outside of the school or department.

We hope that when novice teachers are hired it is because potential was seen in them. We also know that novices often struggle when their ideal of teaching does not match the reality. So when this struggle is apparent, remind novices of the potential that was recognized in them and share how leadership is committed to help them develop. Development may even mean recognizing an outstanding paraprofessional and supporting her development into a special education teacher as she pursues coursework.

Be honest with underperforming teachers. If a teacher's performance is not up to par and the teacher is not doing anything to improve, seriously consider whether that person belongs in the classroom with students. Be honest and share the facts. Certainly follow due process and the school system's policies. One toxic attitude can drain a staff.

Case in Point

Georgia was a teacher who "got by." She was relatively unobtrusive in the school. The problem was that Georgia had been teaching 17 years in the same school system and no one really had anything good or bad to say about her. The most anyone could say was that she was always on time and her room was quiet.

A new principal was assigned to her school and charged folks with engaging students' minds. Georgia's "Read the chapter and answer the questions" lesson plans did not evoke images of actively engaged, critically thinking students. One day her principal sat down in Georgia's classroom during her planning time and shared the schoolwide test results from the previous year which were good, and then she showed Georgia a graph with just her students. Georgia's students were underperforming. It was not good enough to have a disruption-free classroom; students needed to be learning more. Georgia was asked "What else can you do with the students?" Georgia's classes got marginally better, but she needed more of a boost. So, the principal put some structured supports in place for Georgia. By the end of the first semester, the school had a transformed Georgia. Someone had challenged her and held her accountable for what she could do.

Say what needs to be heard. There are realities or conflicts in the school that everyone knows, but may not want to discuss or even acknowledge. Perhaps it is a staff member who frequently is 15 minutes late to work and arrives just before a bell rings for students to enter the building. When murmurings are heard or a teacher is complaining about a colleague ask, "Have you spoken to your colleague yet?" If the answer is no, find out why, and then encourage the teacher to talk to the other person. The teacher may fear offending his colleague or be uncomfortable, so role playing may help. Perhaps the teacher just wants to avoid the conflict all together by placing it on your platter. Perhaps a neutral person is needed to help the parties communicate more effectively. Staff members often will go out of their way to accommodate or avoid the so-called elephant in the school, yet this has the unintended consequence of reducing the effectiveness of the school. So encourage staff members sharing their concerns with their colleagues in a respectful manner, even if it means symbolically holding a staff members' hands.

Create a Tradition with Leadership Development

Every leader is also a follower. A teacher leads students while following the principal who leads a school while following the superintendent. Leadership qualities may be innately within a person or have been developed through the careful mentoring or a "trial by fire."

A review of 25 years of school improvement research found that principals in schools that are improving and achieving invest considerable amounts of time in developing their staff's capabilities (Hallinger & Heck, 1998). The reality in education is that no one person, no matter how enthusiastic and smart, can single-handedly bring about change—one can lead a paradigm shift, but others must buy into it and follow. Effective leaders develop their staff members such that they can confidently "give the authority for making decisions to those closest to the task" (DuFour & Eaker, 1998, p. 186). This empowerment of others comes "by making sure they have the autonomy and the resources that they need to do their jobs well" (Bolman & Deal, 1997). A review of attributes of successful school improvement teams found that the principal developed and supported the leadership capacity of teachers in order to effect team success (Dexter & Turk, 2002). At the school level, for example, teachers are empowered to act and think like leaders in professional learning communities (DuFour

& Eaker). By creating situations that foster leadership and supporting the decisions made by staff members in whom authority was vested, leaders can develop a cadre of future leaders.

Ideas from the Field

Share the floor. Invite formal or informal leaders to present with you. For example, if part of the monthly faculty meeting is an update of how the school is progressing toward its school improvement goal in reading, ask a teacher or the reading specialist to share the data update from the predictor tests. A teacher may share an instructional strategy that she has found particularly useful with students. The presentation venue could also be a local, state, or national conference in which the positive experiences of your school's initiatives are shared with others.

Case in Point

A math department chair was invited to present at a state-level conference on integrating technology into instruction. She asked permission to bring two of her colleagues with her. This was the first time the teachers, one of whom was a first-year novice teacher, had shared examples of what they were doing with other professionals.

Several months later, the novice teacher agreed to present a districtwide workshop on integrating technology into the classroom. She told her department chair that while she had been nervous at the state conference, the response she received from participants gave her the confidence to be willing to lead a presentation. The presentation went well for the 23-year-old teacher.

Two years later, that novice teacher wrote a grant proposal and received a grant of $3,500 to provide professional development and materials to the math teachers in her school. The next year, with merely 4 years of teaching experience she became a department chair in her school district.

Develop leadership capacity. Sharing responsibility and leadership opportunities tells teachers that their expertise is valued. Share with staff members why they would be good at a particular leadership task, or if the staff member has initiated interest, reflect with him or her on why the leadership opportunity would be appropriate. This becomes another form of induction as teachers are introduced to an additional facet of education, the leadership piece. It also serves as a retention component as teachers see a return on their investment in the school.

Provide opportunities for teachers to volunteer. Let teachers know about school needs and leadership opportunities. There may be someone on staff who is interested; just knowing about the need or opportunity may encourage the person to come forward. Additionally, subtle prompting may encourage a teacher to volunteer as the individual may not have realized her potential until the instructional leader helped make the connection between a school or student need and the teacher's skills, knowledge, or ability.

Support staff member initiatives that are aligned to school goals. The great thing about leadership is that you do not have to come up with all the ideas. You can assess proposals to determine if they are feasible for the school, grade level, or subject area. Ideas need not be formally written. If you heard the idea through the grapevine and it has potential, then follow up. Sometimes support is as simple as signing the grant paperwork that the professional has already completed. Other times support may require some investment of time or school resources from you.

Author's Tale
Supporting Professional Growth Benefits School Staff Development

During my fifth year of teaching, I returned to school to work on my master's degree in educational administration. My principal was an excellent model for me of how to build relationships while focusing on school success. In time, the principal became my mentor. Occasionally, she arranged class coverage for me to accompany her to districtwide principals' meetings. We discussed content that I was learning in class and how it applied in our school. She provided opportunities for me to practice leadership skills by asking me, along with other teachers, to lead a staff development initiative at the school. She cultivated new learning experiences because she saw potential in me and my willingness to learn.

—Leslie Grant

Conscientious Retention Efforts

Leadership matters. A recent study found that the top-ranked reason (39.2 %) teachers said that they stayed in their current school was a "supportive school leadership" (Hirsch, 2006, p. 11); 73% of teachers in the same study said that inadequate building-level leadership would influence a decision to change schools or leave the teaching profession. Leaders can increase teacher retention by being "present, positive, and actively engaged in the instructional life of the school" (Johnson & The Project on the Next Generation of Teachers, 2006, p. 15). The 2006 MetLife Survey of the American Teacher (Figure 4.2) interview findings found that many of the strategies suggested by teachers, principals, and college deans to increase teacher retention appeared on all three lists. Two of them (i.e., salaries, school funding) are not within a building-level instructional leaders' control to effect change in most situations, so the cells are gray. However, leaders can implement the other strategies in the graphic.

Figure 4.2. Comparison of the Top Four Strategies To Retain Teachers According to Teachers, Principals, and College Deans

Top 4 Strategies	Teachers (% respondents)	Principals (% respondents)	College Deans (% respondents)
1	Decent Salary (92%)	Decent Salary (88%)	Decent Salary (90%)
2	Increase School System Funding (84%)	Increase School System Funding (84%)	More Respect by Society in General (82%)
3	More Respect by Society in General (82%)	Time to Discuss Educational Issues with Other Teachers (80%)	Increase School System Funding (72%)
4	Better Availability of Needed Resources and Supplies (74%)	More Respect by Society in General (79%)	More Professional Development Opportunities (71%)

Note: Table was created from findings presented in the following study: Metropolitan Life. (2006). *The MetLife survey of the American teacher: Expectations and experiences.* Retrieved October 13, 2006, from www.metlife.com/teachersurvey

Value Staff Input

Taken as a whole, school staffs can have an impressive list of credentials accumulated from years of teaching: career experiences such as engineering, attorney, career military, real estate, and journalism as well as educational and travel opportunities. Good leaders surround themselves with knowledgeable people to keep them informed and to help execute visions to attain goals and objectives. Effective administrators, department chairs, and central office leaders listen to teachers, offer support when needed, but refrain from dominating situations (Billingsley, 2004; Quinn, 2005). Leadership is a balance of leading and knowing when to step back.

When professionals have the skills and abilities to make sound decisions, leaders should encourage this behavior rather than micromanaging teachers' decisions. Several studies have found that the ability to participate in the school decision-making process is valued by teachers (Darling-Hammond & Berry, n.d.; Jorissen, 2002; Perie, Baker, & Whitener, 1997; Quinn, 2005). An Alabama survey found that 75% of teachers who stayed in teaching believed they were empowered to make decisions in their school or classroom (Hirsch, 2006). Given the value professionals place on decision making, it is equally important that leaders support teachers and the decisions they make so long as they are appropriate and well grounded (Billingsley, 2004; Charlotte Advocates for Education, 2004; Gersten, et al., 2005; Perie et al., 1997; Wald, 1998).

Ideas from the Field

Listen. Nothing communicates a valuing of people more than someone's willingness to be quiet and hear what is being said. It may be letting a staff member fume and vent until the person finally articulates the issue at hand. It can be reading an idea submitted to the suggestion box. It may be having an open-door policy where staff members know that they can come and share ideas and concerns with you. People often know what is needed to address a situation or make an initiative even better, and they need leadership to support them. Sometimes folks just want their ideas validated.

Invite staff members to talk to you. If you are the new department chair, the new administrator in the school, the new principal, or the new content area supervisor at the central office, consider sending a letter introducing yourself to your teachers and inviting them to come and have a "get to know you" chat. If may even help to state in the letter times when you are available. Often these discussions not only build goodwill, but let you know what is working and not working well.

Let staff members help each other. Provide opportunities for teachers to talk with each other about their problems and needs. Schedule teams or grade level with common planning periods. Scheduling common planning times for mentors and their teachers has advantages (e.g., can meet) and disadvantages (e.g., need a substitute to cover in order to observe each other). If the content of a faculty meeting can be addressed in a memo, e-mail teachers that small group discussions will be occurring around the specific topics. Recruit teachers to serve as moderators or facilitators for each topic. Let teachers self-select which group they want to join. Refer teachers to each other for discussions.

Use surveys. Check the "temperature of the staff" with a survey or just a short few open-ended questions a couple of times a year. Surveys can support relationships because they demonstrate a valuing of people's perspectives. There are a variety of free surveys available online, ranging from organizational climate to learning styles. Then build on the results of the surveys. Examine the data for themes of specific strengths and weaknesses that large and small groups can address. Share the results with staff and give them a voice in selecting areas to target. It may be advantageous to group faculty members outside of their comfort zones, such as putting different grade levels or department members together so that diverse perspectives are generated during the activity of selecting the target areas. This not only generates multiple perspectives, but also encourages staff members to interact with others with whom they might not ordinarily work because of compartmentalization in the school.

Talk about money. School budgets are small and department budgets are even smaller, but there may be an appropriate opportunity to let staff have input on how funds are spent.

Case in Point

The science department received $3.00 per student to purchase laboratory equipment and supplies each year. The department chair was responsible for submitting the order. She used some of the money to purchase schoolwide equipment and then told teachers to look at their current supplies and determine what materials they wanted to order. She also included the special education self-contained teachers, giving them a budget based on the number of students they taught. It was the teachers' option whether to pool resources, as some did, or to submit individual orders. This simple action gave the teachers control of what was spent on behalf of the students they would teach during the upcoming year.

Share the Glory

School leaders are under tremendous pressure to motivate their staffs to perform incredible feats of student learning. At every level of leadership, there is someone to whom answers must be given. School principals often are concerned about the school report cards that are published in the newspaper, typically with the principal's name. Directors of instruction have superintendents. The superintendent has the school board, community, and state superintendent. The list is endless, but at the foundation of all the learning is the teacher and the student. Communicating the message that teachers are important and valued by professionals for the work that they perform is part of sharing the glory (Charlotte Advocates for Education, 2004; Darling-Hammond & Berry, n.d.; Inman & Marlow, 2004; Jorissen, 2002; Wald, 1998). A nationally representative sample of over 1,000 teachers revealed that 82% of respondents felt that the principal showing appreciation for teachers' work was very important (Metropolitan Life, 2006). President Harry S. Truman said, "It is amazing what you can accomplish if you do not care who gets the credit." The reality is that this works so long as the leader is willing to acknowledge those who did the work.

Ideas from the Field

Celebrate what is good. If a staff member had an idea that was put into practice and netted the intended results, acknowledge the person. Acknowledgements can be as simple as a note "Caught you being good" or more elaborate such as a take-off of the academy awards in which staff members receive certificates noting accomplishments or expertise. Many schools that have marquees on the school could display congratulatory messages. Some candy bars even have names that sound like rewards: most leaders can not give spot bonuses (monetary rewards in businesses), but they can give someone a 100,000 Grand or an extra Payday—with appropriately named candy bars.

Talk about your staff in positive terms. If someone asks you "How is it going?" take the opportunity to tell about something wonderful you observed in a classroom and use the staff member's name. Communities, even in large cities are small, and comments often get back to the person that was spoken about, so make sure your comments are ones you want them to hear.

Recap

- Choose teachers deliberately, not out of necessity: Think of ways to get the candidate you want out of the applicant pool and into your worksite.
- Select the lead team: Build a core team for your school or district, so that everyone is working towards the same mission and vision.
- Know your people as you assign responsibilities: Make deliberate well-thought-out staffing choices.
- Have your staff understand each others' strengths and weaknesses: Acknowledge that everyone has attributes and needs, so by working together we can achieve more than by working alone.
- Create a tradition with leadership development: Recognize, mentor, and provide opportunities for your followers to assume leadership roles.
- Value staff input: Seek and consider faculty expertise, opinions, and reflections.
- Share the glory: Identify ways to involve staff and faculty members in the positive accolades the school may be receive or the you may receive on behalf of the school.

Reflection Moment

Take 5 to 8 minutes to think about the following questions.

- To what degree do I get the teachers I want for the school and keep them?
- What do I do to maximize the potential and performance of the teachers with whom I work?
- How do I identify staff needs and respond to them?
- Which one of the *Ideas from the Field* could I try this week? Use in the future?

5
Influence: Leaders Positively Affecting Teachers

When one thinks of power, one might think in terms of power in a negative sense. And, history and our own life experiences support that power can be used in a way that is heavy-handed or viewed as aristocratic and arbitrary in nature. School leaders, like leaders in history or contemporary leaders in our community, do hold "power." Power is the overarching term that basically means there is an ability to get results (Bolman & Deal, 1997). There are several variations of power that all revolve around some distinct feature that allows one to get things done. These features may be just as easily divided between *authority* and *influence*. Authority can be defined as delegated power, in other words, an administrator has "power" merely because of his or her position. This chapter, however, focuses on *influence* which may or may not accompany authority and is most likely developed by leaders themselves. We choose to emphasize power's ability to *positively influence* the behaviors and actions of others. More important, however, the leader also influences people's attitudes, and a change in attitude will lead to changes in behaviors and actions (Ashley, 2008).

The ultimate aim of education and of any educational program or any professional's position is to make a difference in the lives of students, specifically to ensure that students leave schools with the knowledge and skills they need to be successful. Students are, after all, the reason why schools exist.

Do school leaders make a difference in how much and how well students learn? Do they make a difference in how effective schools are in meeting the needs of students? Whereas it is difficult to demonstrate a direct link between student achievement and the school leader (Hallinger & Heck, 1998), a review of research indicates that indirect links can be made (Stronge, 2008). For example, research supports that school leaders can influence school cultures and school cultures directly contribute to school effectiveness (Leithwood & Jantzi, 1999).

Making a difference depends on the *positive influence* that a school leader has on those with whom the leader works on a daily basis and those with whom the leader comes into contact with on a less frequent basis but who impact the educational process nonetheless. The astute school leader knows how to use influence both within her domain of influence (e.g. hiring qualified teachers) and outside of her domain of influence (e.g. a news story being published about the school in the local media). The school leader also understands the importance of making decisions that are in the best interests of students and considers the possible effects of those decisions on all involved. Efforts are made to influence others through practical means such as being visible in school hallways, at staff meetings and planning, monitoring, observing, and scheduling school programs.

Educational leaders' influence is achieved through (a) respected leadership; (b) deliberate decisions; and (c) concerted efforts (see Figure 5.1).

Respected Leadership

In order for any leader to be able to positively influence the behaviors and actions of others, she must be respected. The word *respect* connotes a variety of meanings. Respect is tied to trust, support, and competence (Tschannen-Moran, 2004). Respect also means acceptance as a leader, which in turn provides opportunities for the leader to indeed influence others (Friedkin & Slater, 1994). In studies of business performance, higher

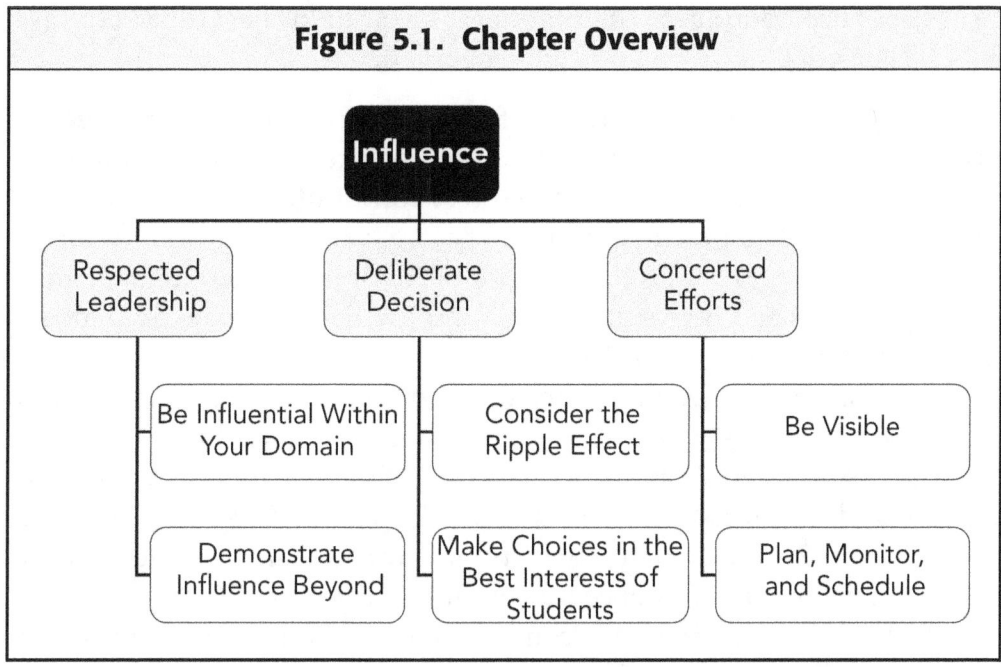

Figure 5.1. Chapter Overview

levels of trust are associated with the relationship that the employee and the leader have, which then leads to increased business performance (Douglas & Zivnuska, 2008). A leader's influence is profound.

School leaders affect those within their domain and beyond their domain. For a building administrator, one might consider the school building the "domain." The leader also influences students, teachers, staff, and parents. And, an administrator can influence those at the district level and at the state level as well as the community at large.

Be Influential Within Your Domain

Any school leader has the ability to directly influence the work of educational professionals with whom they work either in a supervisory or a collegial capacity. According to one study, employees were realistic about what their supervisors could and could not do within the constraints of the organization; however, employees favorably responded when their supervisors' actions

- made work more interesting
- promoted teamwork

- enhanced bonding with other employees (Nohria, Groysberg, & Lee, 2008).

In fact, employee survey results from two large studies identified the need to bond, "to create a culture that promotes teamwork, collaboration, openness, and friendship," as the largest contributor to employee commitment to the organization (Nohria et al., p. 82). Regardless of your job title, seeking opportunities to influence the establishment of relationships among teachers and between yourself and teachers will pay dividends in increased employee satisfaction.

Consider the effects on teacher retention mentioned in Chapter 4. In a survey of teachers who left the profession in England in 2002, 34.5% rated stress as a very important factor in their decision to leave the profession, and 20% rated the way the school is run as important (Smithers & Robinson, 2003). Clearly, the school leader influences the way the school is run *and* can influence the amount of stress felt by staff.

The building administrator comes into direct contact with school faculty and staff, students at the school, and parents of students. Directors of instruction work on a continuing basis with curriculum specialists or coordinators and staff development specialists. But influence is not a one-way street in which school leaders influence those over which they have supervisory capacity. Influence can run up the line and staff. Administrators can have an impact on their superiors.

As stated earlier, the main point of our existence as educators is that we have students to educate. School leaders can influence the lives of students in indirect ways by influencing those who work with students. A building level administrator works with teachers on a daily basis and influences the social network and people within the building. Indeed, "a major impact of principal efforts is to produce changes in people" (Hallinger & Heck, 1998, p. 175). Principals can influence what teachers teach and how they teach. This can be done by becoming a central part of the discussion in matters of school governance. Friedkin and Slater (1994) found that there are essentially three ways principals influence schools.

1. Serve in an advisory capacity to teachers to solve problems at the classroom level, leading to improved teaching and learning.

2. Become a source of advice across teachers and grade levels by being available and centrally located, encouraging a common understanding of thoughts and expectations.
3. Gain social acceptance and respect, contributing to the administrator's ability to problem solve

Central to these ways of effectiveness are accessibility of the leader, attentiveness of the leader, and collaborative problem solving and decision making (Friedkin & Slater, 1994). Mutual respect is a key to this influence. "The nature of supervision in schools should focus on helping, not directing teachers to improve their teaching" (Hoy & Miskel, 2001, p. 221). Teachers and others in a subordinate role need to be worked *with* and not worked *on*.

Influence does not only work down the line and staff but also "up" the line and staff. A director of instruction for elementary level can have influence on the assistant superintendent for instruction in making decisions about which reading program to implement at the K–2 level. A building level administrator may influence a human resource director's decision to offer early hire to an outstanding teaching candidate. A teacher leader may convince an administrator that a group of teachers should attend a local literacy conference. The ability to influence those higher up also has added benefits for the relationship between the administrator and those that work with the administrator. For example, a study of two very different schools showed how the relationship between the building level administrator and the superintendent could possibly affect teachers at the school (Glascock & Taylor, 2001). Figure 5.2

Figure 5.2. Views of Superintendent/Principal Relationship				
	Teacher Engagement	Effect of Principal on Teachers' Work	Teachers' View of Relationship Between Superintendent and Principal	Principals' View of Relationship With Superintendent
School A	Moderate	Moderate	Neutral to positive	Distant
School B	High	High	Positive	Close Professional

shows these two different schools, the views of teachers at the school, and the principal's relationship with the superintendent.

In school B, the teachers perceive their relationship as strictly positive while teachers in School A perceive the relationship between the principal and the superintendent as distant. In School B, the teachers perceive themselves as engaged and the administrator has a good rapport among staff. The principal enjoys a close professional relationship with the superintendent and often consults with central office staff. Clearly, the relationship is key to getting things done.

The relationship can also be key in acting on the behalf of others. When administrators can exert influence on superiors and use it to help those in the trenches, the administrators earn trust and respect (Hoy & Miskel, 2001). This willingness and ability to use influence on superiors can also have an indirect effect on student learning—by increasing teacher efficacy. A study of elementary teachers found that teachers had a greater sense of self-efficacy if the administrator could indeed make things happen (Hoy & Woolfolk, 1993). Imagine a group of teachers who would like to use a historical novel to make connections between literature and social studies. They need a class set of the novels but have no money. The teachers have been working with the language arts curriculum coordinator to plan this interdisciplinary unit, but the school does not have the money to make the needed purchase. How disappointing for the teachers! Now imagine that the language arts coordinator met with the director of instruction regarding the situation and a classroom set of novels shows up at the classroom door. The teachers know that the language arts coordinator is in their corner and is committed to assisting them in making learning meaningful for students. A research study that examined 17 studies that demonstrated impact of professional development on student achievement found five leadership dimensions in these studies. Among these was ensuring that teachers have the resources they need (Robinson & Timperley, 2007).

Ideas from the Field

Be attentive—see what happens. This is also called situational awareness. In other words know what is going on in the building with the people. Whether the school leader is giving praise to a teacher for delivery of a great lesson, jumping for joy with a teacher because of the high test scores, or sitting with a teacher and listening to her share the heartache of going through a divorce, all of these things are very important for supervisors to be aware of.

Be attentive to the good things and praise accordingly. Be attentive to what is going on in the lives of your staff and demonstrate a little caring. For a personal example, the office received a phone call for a teacher that her dad was rushed to the emergency room, the principal went to the room to get the teacher and offered to have someone to drive her to the hospital. An instructional example is when the assistant principal informally visits classrooms, debriefs with the staff, and then shares highlights to the rest of the faculty about the great things she saw in particular classrooms. This lets the staff know that the assistant principal is attentive to instruction and also shares to the others what good practices look like. Being attentive to the needs and quality of the school faculty often gains more mileage and respect in the long run than just pushing to get the job done as folks often want to be noticed in a positive way.

Be clear. School leaders are expected to provide educational direction. Be explicit and clear about expectations and how they relate to the vision. Reinforce the message through your actions. For example, sit in on key meetings, continually put the needs of the school in the forefront of the work that is to be accomplished by applying the "is this good for students?" test, and work toward the desired direction by examining data, reflecting on student outcomes, and assessing the course of action pursued by the school and its faculty.

Work together. There is a saying that many hands make lighter work; by working together the overall load is still the same, but it is distributed among the stakeholders such that no one is overloaded. Further collaboration increases ownership and investment in success. Working together also builds skills, such as considering when to walk beside someone versus when to let them muddle for a time alone. A new teacher once commented that there were many times when she understood what people were saying, but she needed to know what the desired outcome looked like, so having the safety net of interaction is beneficial. By working together, there are opportunities to question, hypothesize, gain insight, and reflect.

Case in Point

    A principal once commented that her real gift was asking the right questions. Often people looked to her for an answer, but she did not have all the answers. However, she could ask the person questions, and depending on the response, her follow-up question would further clarify the issue. The principal commented that often the wise professionals with whom she worked had the answers; they just needed help separating them from all the distractions.

Be accessible. Faculty need to know that their leadership is accessible and is willing and open to being approached. When assigning a task, let the person or committee know that you are willing to help or answer questions. For example, if a report is due and the report writer has not previously written one, tell him or her to e-mail it to you the week before it is due so that you can provide feedback. This way the person knows up front that you are invested. Other strategies include the following:

- communication liaisons—These individuals are especially useful in large settings. They are identified and designated to engage in conversations with leadership. For example, this may be a grade-level chair who is the voice of the grade. Of course anyone can speak up; the liaisons are the ones who also speak for those who are reluctant to speak.
- open-door policy
- designated office hours—Many leaders strive to be out of their offices and in the school. This can have the unintended consequence of making it harder to reach the administrator or department chair for one-to-one conversations. If there are designated times that staff know that the person is available, then they can drop by or schedule a meeting.

Being perceived as accessible is more challenging if there is a lack of a relationship between the teacher and leader. One can have an open-door policy, but if the staff is afraid, not trusting, or has heard stories of someone being turned away, then they will not come, even if the door is open. Even though staff members are professionals too, the leader should reach out to staff, such as meeting them in their classrooms, greeting them in the halls, and building a relationship from scratch. In attending to the people first and the business of school second, leadership is modeling that people are valued.

Be a resource. Share research and articles. Perhaps create a wiki page for staff with articles to read and questions for staff to consider that are aligned to the staff development focus(es) for the year. Wiki pages are a helpful resource as teachers can review comments and interact asynchronously. Recommend books for a collegial study. Know and use your connections to benefit the staff and school. For example, civic organizations often seek local groups to support. Why not have the school leader's club support your school? Call for reinforcements when necessary whether it be from the central office or another entity. For example the state department of education may have outreach offices to help school personnel at little to no cost with specific issues such as special education or homelessness. A final suggestion is to coach folks through new experiences, providing them with support to be successful as they navigate unfamiliar terrain. Basically don't sit back and wait for things to happen—make things happen!

Case in Point

This occurred nearly 15 years ago, but it is a good story. The school had received a full computer lab (30 computers with Internet capability and printers). The school was not scheduled to be wired for Internet until the following year due to personnel constraints; however, the school system had prepurchased the necessary wiring and warehoused it. Luckily, one of the assistant principals had a neighbor in the army who worked in a unit that wired offices and set up computers on the base. The neighbor brought volunteers from his unit to the school to wire the building. On one Saturday morning, military men and women crawled around, climbed up ladders, fished line through the ceilings, and got the Internet lines hooked up. The lab was operational—a year ahead of schedule.

Demonstrate Influence Beyond

Administrators due to their direct involvement in a community can have a far reaching influence on the greater community, which in turn influences education. "It is imperative for professionals entrusted with people's children to inspire confidence in parents and communities, to project an image of quality" (Schmoker, 2006, p. 30). School leaders interact with a multitude of people who can then influence others. Consider the following list:

- Taxpayers without school-aged children
- Taxpayers with school-aged children who attend private school
- Local newspaper and television reporters
- Community leaders, such as those in local Kiwanis, Lion's Club, Junior Women's League, National Urban League
- Community agencies, such as local social services, nonprofit organizations that champion the causes of children

School leaders must take every opportunity to share the positive news of what is happening in schools. So many times the public hears the negative: low test scores, gun found in student locker, kindergartner expelled for kissing another student, and the list goes on. The public needs, and most likely prefers, to hear the positive: a fourth grader wins an essay contest on patriotism, middle school band students win local competition, high school football team goes on to state, elementary school student's artwork selected as nationalist final, and the list goes on. School leaders acknowledge the negative and make sure that others know about the positive.

Ideas from the Field

Make "stuff" happen. If you have a great staff focused on kids and learning, a real opportunity to shine is when you make a hope a reality. Teachers know that schools are not flush with cash. So when a request is made for the purchase of something that really will help students and learning, seriously consider if the request can be granted. Get the specific request in writing (title of the resource/equipment and cost). Check with the bookkeeper for any unexpended funds that could be consolidated to fund the request. Check with the central office supervisor, call the PTA, or as one principal said, "Beg from all places."

Protect the teachers' time. Schools contain captive audiences. So deciding who is given access to teachers and students warrants attention. Financial institutions want to share retirement vehicles, education companies want to share new gadgets and resources, nonprofits may have a unit or initiative they want to share, and this only touches the tip of the iceberg of parties approaching leadership for "just a moment of time." A key question is "Does this group further the instructional focus of the school?" Some of the approaching groups truly are of interest to a majority of teachers, but they may not meet this test. One strategy is to let the representative come on a teacher workday and offer a 20-minute program complete with breakfast or snacks, so teachers can opt into attending. Another strategy for granting access is to let representatives into the building during lunch time, so teachers can meet with them in the faculty lounge.

Be prepared for the public. Send pictures and press releases to the newspaper (or go through the school system's public affairs office if there is an established protocol). Highlight positives on the school marquee sign, in the school newsletters, and on the school Web site. Host celebrations to welcome the parents and families into the building such as receptions for student achievements and honor roll. Always have a couple of items about the school, teachers, or students that are extremely positive so that when asked about the school, you can give a genuine and targeted response. These items can be highlighted for new staff members, parents, school board members, and other parties. This is especially helpful when something negative has occurred at the school and the press is knocking at the door. Certainly answering questions directly and accurately as possible is important. Working in the positives of the school to the conversation can change a negative story into a positive view of the school.

Case in Point

A middle school principal received a call from a news reporter. The news reporter wanted to come and interview the principal because the school had an infestation of red fire ants, which can be quite annoying and dangerous! The administrator could see the news truck out of his window as he talked on the telephone. The principal agreed that they could come, but requested that they stow their cameras and report to the main office as cameras coming into a middle school would cause a disruption in the hallway. The TV crew knew they had access and understood the importance of not causing a disruption in the running of the middle school. This also afforded the principal the opportunity to "manage" the crew. He toured them around the school and spoke with the reporter. He conveyed that the ant issue was being taken care of, the school and its occupants were safe, and that the school had some outstanding state test scores to be proud of. He even threw in some humor with a "lords of the ants" dance.

When a newspaper reporter came out to cover the story, the principal continued to share his key points: safe school and high achievement. At the principal's invitation, the reporter returned on a teacher workday to speak with teachers in the library about upcoming instructional activities that might have been of interest to the public, and nearly two pages of ideas were generated. The reporter returned three more times to the suburban school for "school interest stories" that highlighted the middle school teachers and their students in a very positive way.

Deliberate Decisions

School leaders make many decisions throughout the day. Many situations such as a water break in the boys' bathroom require a quick response. Most situations, however, allow the leader to take into account the factors in making the decision and include others in the decision process, then come to a final decision. Here is a classic model for decision making:

- Identify and analyze a problem
- Develop and evaluate alternatives
- Choose and implement the best solution

These steps to decision making are very simple yet offer a systematic way of approaching situations that may arise. However, whether a decision must be made in a reactionary manner or can be analyzed, the mission and vision discussed in Chapter 2 will provide the foundation for any decisions that are made. When decisions align with the vision and mission, they are deliberate whether they are made in reaction to a crisis situation or not. A leader's ability to lead and influence others may depend on how decisions are made.

Consider the Ripple Effect

Race horses have blinders near their eyes so that they only see straight ahead. This ensures that they keep their eyes on the prize, which is the finish line. Such a practice is commonplace and indeed necessary. For an educational leader, having blinders on when making decisions can lead to disastrous results. A school leader who puts blinders on and drops a pebble into a body of water may only see the pebble hit the water. What he doesn't see are the ripples coming from the pebble. School leaders must consider the possible effects of those decisions and weigh the positive and negative effects against the intended outcome. Senge (2006) calls this "systems thinking." For example, if the decision is made to move a teacher to a new grade level, what are the possible ramifications of that decision? Is the teacher willing to move? How will the move affect the current grade level? How will the move affect the new grade level team? These ripple effects of decisions must be considered.

Another aspect in the ripple effect to consider is the informal leaders in the school. What are the reactions of the informal leaders to the decisions that were made? Were they involved in the decision-making process? Should they have been involved? There are teacher leaders who do not have any authority *over* their colleagues, yet they do exert a great deal of influence *with* their fellow teachers. Influential individuals seek to create conditions in which their opinion is valued and they think like a partner while operating within the boss' preferred mode—collaboration or hierarchy, for example (Cohen & Bradford, 1990). Think of a teacher whom you know is well-respected by colleagues, gets amazing results with students, works well with parents, and whose input is sought for various initiatives from curriculum planning to evaluation system design. This person is influential in both his or her immediate zone of responsibility (e.g., students and parents) and also beyond (e.g., colleagues, superiors). Such teachers are barometers for how changes will be perceived in the school, they are well connected, and they consistently act in the best interest of students and the school. Get the informal leaders involved and invested. Influence is about connectional power—the ripple effect.

Ideas From the Field

Cause ripples. How do amazingly effective leaders get the job done? They are passionate, they are persistent, they have a direction, and they provide clear leadership. In schools where progress is evident, staffs are happy, and kids are engaged, there is a leader working *behind* the scene, *on* the scene, and *in front of* the scene. Results are readily seen and staff are willing to follow as they know there is a positive, powerful, and influential force. This is all about action, not words. People see the ripples and choose to jump into the water.

Establish "touch points." Standards, data, and needs are common refrains in schools: *Touch points* are items that keep leaders in touch with the landscape of the school. Know your metrics for success, progress, and evaluation of proposals. Use those touch points to guide decisions and base choices. Consider where they will intersect to help identify added bonuses or potential concerns of a decision.

Talk to staff about where the students are and where they need to be.
Most employees in schools get "it." The focus is on students and their instruction. If students would benefit from a different or new instructional strategy and teachers need professional development, then there is a push for training. For example, tech savvy students respond to blogs, wiki posts, probeware, software programs and hardware, so staff need to keep up with what students are learning on their own or have a desire to learn. Continually engage in dialogue about where you are and how you are going to continue the journey. This dialogue may be about instruction, school climate, school safety, scheduling, assessment, or a host of other related items.

Case in Point

An administrator decides to move teachers in a middle school so that teams are closer in proximity. The close proximity will reduce the need for students to travel farther to change classes and allows for teachers to quickly talk with each other if needed. This is a logical and sound move, which should be simple except for the fact that one of the classrooms in question was a professional development room that was turned into classroom when enrollment increased a few years ago. The former professional development room has more bells and whistles than other classroom, and a teacher will need to be moved out of that room. The administrator knows that the teacher will resist the move, but discusses the decision with the teacher. The teacher is not happy but understands the reasons. The administrator makes the move knowing that the teacher may hold some hard feelings, but at least she is not surprised when she shows up at the start of the school year, and all of her materials are in a different room.

Make Choices in the Best Interests of Students

Students should be at the center of any decision that is made in schools. This is a value that a school leader must hold and expect of others. Consider the following two actions: The water break in the girls' bathroom must be fixed so that girls can go to the bathroom! The teachers' classrooms must be moved so that students have less distance to travel between classes. In each of these examples, students are at the center. How will this decision affect children? There are situations such as the first example where the choice must be immediate; whereas, the second must be deliberate.

Two attributes associated with effective principals are their ability to (a) respond (e.g., supportive, empowering, listening, working well with others, letting others experience success) and (b) demand (e.g., high and clear expectations with feedback, confidence, assertiveness, decisive, challenging the norm). These two forces working in concert can improve a school or maintain upward momentum (Dinham, 2007). The efforts of these two forces can be reciprocal as "being responsive through recognizing, empowering, and meeting the needs of others, leaders create an expectation, desire, and even obligation for staff and students to perform at a higher level with the frequently cited observation that people 'don't want to let [the leader] down," (Dinham, p. 273). Leadership focuses on supporting students, collaboration, teacher learning, trust, and engagement. A culture of success provides the nutrients necessary to grow strong relationships.

Ideas From the Field

Invite staff to make their personal framework student-focused. As a leader you really can control and change only yourself, but you can affirm, invite, or inspire others to make decisions in the best interests of students. Ways to do this are the following:

- Encourage staff members to think about why they chose education. Why this vocation?
- Examine academic data with departments or grade levels.
- Review student data (e.g., attendance, referral) with counselors and assistant principals and share summaries with teachers.
- Meet with teachers during content or grade level meetings to discuss upcoming lessons.
- Be excited and show passion about learning and students.
- Provide extrinsic motivators where it benefits staff to put students first.
- Ask people, "Is this good for kids?"

Case in Point

A teacher leader attended a conference which stressed the importance of focusing on children. The keynote speaker had everyone fired up after the banquet! The teacher leader came up with the idea to create small posters and business-sized cards with the question, "How will this decision affect children?" She gave the posters and cards to the teachers and asked them to think about this question whenever they are about to make a decision about what to teach, how to work through a difficult situation with a student, or whatever situation may arise.

Support teachers in putting their children first. Many teachers have families and children. Expect teachers to be involved in their own children's lives, even if the involvement is during school hours. A related benefit is that the public will see that the teachers value their child's education—in essence modeling good parenting skills.

Teachers sometimes stress and struggle with the conflicting needs of meeting the needs of their children on one hand and the needs of their students on the other. A teacher may need coverage to leave school for an hour and a half to attend a child's honor roll celebration, meet with the child's teacher, or watch a preschooler's class play. Just imagine the internal guilt a teacher may have in telling her 4-year-old that "Mommy can not come see you be a daisy in the school play because Mommy has to teach," and then during the time the play is being performed, the teacher is likely having thoughts about her young child not having a parent to watch her performance. Teachers typically are judicious with their requests for coverage if this is allowed and most appreciative that they have a relationship where they can say, "I need to do this for my child." In this case, leadership chooses to recognize that the best interests of the student may not always directly involve the student in their school. However, in meeting teachers' personal needs to parent, leadership and students are getting a more content and focused teacher.

Concerted Efforts

Change in others does not occur by happenstance. Well, this is not necessarily the case. A child may learn not to touch a hot stove by touching a hot stove. The change in behavior happened but it was certainly not planned! Many times a parent can tell the child that the stove is "hot" and the child gets it. This is the influence of the parent. Likewise, school leaders can have influence on others by making concerted efforts to do so. The relationship between school leaders and those with whom they work and have the capacity and the opportunity to influence is much different from the parent-child relationship. Kouzes and Posner (2002) champion five practices that define exemplary leaders. These practices are listed below (Figure 5.3) along with examples of how these might be seen in education. These practices can be accomplished only if the school leader makes plans to influence others and is visible to others.

Be Visible

Visibility is a crucial part of being influential. Indeed, availability and accessibility are cited as two keys to affecting others' beliefs and practices (Glascock & Taylor, 2001). "Research shows us that apart from anything

Figure 5.3. Exemplary Leadership Practices and Examples	
Practice[a]	Case in Point Example
Modeling	An administrator walks the halls during class changes and student arrival/dismissal because she wants her staff to also "be in the halls" during these times.
Inspiring	A superintendent works with a group of community and school leaders to envision the school district in 10 years and to plan how to realize that vision.
Challenging	A teacher leader shares reading achievement data with the third grade reading team and brainstorms with them about how to get every student to learn, from bringing up students who are below-grade-level readers to providing enriching experiences for advance readers.
Enabling	A mathematics curriculum specialist provides the materials necessary for teachers to use manipulatives in the classroom.
Encouraging	A mentor teacher gives a pep talk to a new teacher who had a bad day. The mentor shares the growth that she has observed in the teacher and speaks of continued development.

[a]The practices were identified by Kouzes and Posner, 2002.

else (e.g., what you say, what you do, how you look), just being present in a place or at an event has an enormous impact on how teachers and students conduct themselves" (McEwan, 2003, p. 70). Visibility within the school walls is key to influencing those within the leader's domain, but visibility outside school walls is key to influencing those outside of the leader's domain. A school leader may attend community organization meetings, sporting events, or the county fair. In each of these events, the leader has the opportunity to influence others' views of the school and of the school district.

Ideas From the Field

Treat others as you want to be treated. Often leaders are observed and do not even know it. People expect a higher standard from their leaders and when they do not get it, they are disappointed or worse, they feel disenfranchised. It seems reasonable to be observed when one is in a school. So if a teacher happens to observe another teacher being rude to you and you are calmly addressing the situation, your stock will go up. But what about out of school? If you are observed being rude to a store clerk, it is not that "Harry Mann" was rude; rather it is "Principal Mann" who was rude. Just be mindful of treating others as you would like to be treated.

Be seen and heard by influential people. Go to school board meetings, if possible, when students from your school are getting awards or making presentations. Attend events where the superintendent and central office supervisors are in attendance. Networking at professional conferences with colleagues whom you may not get much face time "back home" is an opportunity. Then, at a national conference, you are the familiar face. Have positive messages about the school, work of the teachers, and student progress to share—short and memorable stories. As a teacher leader, be visible to your administrators by attending school events, participating or leading professional developments, or inviting the administrator to do the welcome of a professional development session.

Attend school events. Being present, accessible, and observed at school events helps to build relationships with teachers as well as students and their families, the community, and central office personnel—in short, anyone else who is also at the event. As a teacher leader, you may be able to attend all school events related to your department or grade level. As an administrator, you can not realistically attend all functions and meetings, although many administrators try to make at least an appearance. Principals already divide up event coverage with their assistant principals to ensure that there is an administrator present at school events, but there may be an activity for which you were specifically invited or really wish you could attend, but can not. Tell folks that you will not be there, and if possible send an affirming message. For example, if your son's baseball game happens to be scheduled at the same time as the after-school basketball awards, then tell the sponsor the reason and wish attendees well at the banquet during the afternoon announcements. This gives the sponsor something to say to parents and students to which they can relate.

Case in Point

Before a PTA meeting started and folks were milling around, a parent asked her fellow parents and the teacher who was standing with them how they knew if the principal was doing a good job. Quickly the parents responded and the teacher agreed that a good principal attended everything. When the parent asked how attendance at school events made a better principal, there was not a definite answer. However, the message was clear; people want to see their leaders at functions in which the stakeholder is invested.

Plan, Monitor, and Schedule

A sure way to work toward changing people's behaviors and attitudes is to plan for how that change might take place. In other words, "what gets measured gets done." For example, in influencing what teachers teach Glatthorn (2000) recommends that school leaders develop specific plans, manage priorities, and control their time so that the program can be monitored. Researchers examining the relationships between leadership behaviors and levels of shared decision making found a significant correlation between planning and providing teachers with the resources and support to carry out their work (Leech & Fulton, 2008). In other words, if the structure is not in place to provide teachers and students with what they need to succeed, the leader loses influence with both groups.

Planning makes teachers' jobs possible. Planning, monitoring, and scheduling ensure success by "translating the abstract vision and goals of an initiative into concrete explanations of what is required" (Robinson & Timperley, 2007, p. 256). If teachers are trying new strategies, school leaders can see if these strategies are working by getting into the classrooms, talking with the teachers, and monitoring student performance. In order to get into classrooms and talk to teachers, the school leader must schedule this time into the day; otherwise the leader's time will not be her own!

Ideas From the Field

Develop long-range plans for the year. Cycle from one academic year to the next, such as from July 1 through June 30 during plan development. Put the obvious on the school calendar: holidays, testing dates, then start to fill it in with your leadership team (if a principal) or teachers (if a teacher leader). Include professional development offerings, names of key people to involve, and follow up with getting commitments early. Review the long-range plans periodically and tweak as necessary.

Designate a monitoring system. If you expect, then inspect. Identify what you will be watching to ensure the work of the school, department, or grade gets done. School improvement plans or goal-setting forms usually identify the measures; it is up to the individual to be accountable in reviewing the items. So take those measures and, during the course of your day, actively look for them in the data that is reviewed, and in the conversations that are held.

Case in Point

Data is available in almost paralyzing abundance. In an effort to organize and focus teachers' attention on data, school leadership made educational data analysis part of the dialogue that teachers had with each other and their administrators. The initiative was designed to support teachers in analyzing what students are being taught and are learning. Teachers had large three-ring notebooks to assist them in organizing materials in which they maintained copies of the following:

- state testing blueprints, testing vocabulary necessary to decoding the blueprints, and state testing cut scores
- curriculum and associated curriculum frameworks
- testing and benchmark data on each student, including intervention tracking sheets for student progress.

The binder also contained monthly articles to read as a department and a staff development calendar. Teachers reviewed weekly data and brainstormed ways to improve student learning with their administrator and/or department chair. In addition, the teachers met every other day about plans. They considered what students were learning and what skills and knowledge needed additional supports. The next step was to provide the supports and assess the success of the interventions. The result were teacher-initiated actions such as periodically switching classes based on skills that students needed, "power hour" of targeted instruction on a single concept with struggling students, and after-school "cool schools" for more intensive and prolonged additional instructional time. When there is this level of collaboration among a team of teachers, there is no greater high for an administrator. The educational analysis process created a situation and a focus by which the teachers became a cohesive group that took ownership for student learning.

Use a daily schedule. A daily schedule whether on a handheld devise, a to-do list, or a daily calendar is an invaluable tool for organizing what needs to occur and what would be nice to get done. It serves as an advance organizer for the day's activities.

Encourage others. Oral, written, and nonverbal affirmation and encouragement help to keep staff members motivated. It may be a quick note jotted on a trusty blue pad or quickly clicked into an electronic handheld device and e-mailed. The little pad of paper is handy as one can pull it out of a pocket and scrawl a note before another pressing issue arises. The notes can easily be placed in teachers' boxes and in time, if the same type of paper is used, people will associate the note with good news.

Recap

- School leaders can have an effect on students by influencing those who work with them through high expectations.
- Deliberate decisions must take into account the effects of the decisions; most important are the effects on students.
- Positive influence must be planned for and in line with the organization's vision, mission, and core values.
- A school leader can influence those outside of schools by being visible in the community.

Reflection Moment

Take 3 to 8 minutes to think about the following questions.

- How much influence do I have in people's attitudes and behaviors, both within my work environment and outside of the work environment?

- Looking at Figure 5.3, which leadership practice is my strength and which one is my weakness? How can I influence people within my own work environment using these practices?
- Which one of the *Ideas From the Field* could I try this week? Use in the future?

6

Conclusion: Relationships Matter.

You have to build relationships with your staff, and rely on those relationships.

> Bob Goerke, Oregon's Distinguished Principal
> in 1999 as cited by Paglin, 2000, p. 2

The chapter's title has a period at the end. The bottom line is that relationships matter, period. There is no exclamation point because the statement is not excitement or surprise, just fact. Schools are made of individual people. But individually, people cannot have the success achieved through *relationships* between people (Fullan, 2001). Fundamentally, leadership is about relationships.

Benefits and Challenges in Building Relationships

Sports provide numerous examples of the power of relationships. For example, every spring Little League Baseball goes into high gear, and many leagues have a rule that everyone gets to play. The coach, players, and families rally together as part of a team, and the coach's vision is that each individual player will become a team player, nurturing care for the game and for each other. Therefore, the purpose of the team is to teach children how to play baseball and how to be team players so that the team performs well and each individual player improves his or her game. By practicing together, reflecting on performance (in other words, thinking about their game), responding to feedback, and playing with heart, the team will experience success—perhaps even winning the championship. The key is for the coach to work with the players and parents as a team. The coach cannot do it alone. A positive relationship must exist among all stakeholders.

Effective leaders recognize and/or create situations in which relationships can flourish. They recognize that relationships may be influenced by working conditions, personnel, or a host of other factors that complicate matters. Yet, leaders persevere in developing relationships as they know that their influence is more effective when there are solid relationships.

Relationships take time to establish and maintain. The Little League Baseball team did not work in unison when taking the field the first time. In fact, 5-year-olds often look like insects swarming toward a ball until they learn the game and how to rely on each other. Candid feedback, a willingness to work together, and meeting on a regular basis resulted in progress. If a team does not practice, their performance diminishes. The same is true of relationships. Even a good relationship can become better with practice, and inattention may cause even a great relationship to languish. A marginal relationship can certainly be improved as well. Begin with what is common, the commitment of most teachers to the academic well-being of their students.

In a standards-based, accountability-driven context, enhancing relationships may seem like a waste of time. Yet the dividends far outweigh any costs. Good relationships benefit staff, enhance school climate, reduce stress, and create support systems. All of these in turn result in a better learning environment to foster student academic growth.

Validating Relationships

In sports, the validation of relationships is readily seen in performance improvement, trophies, and player interactions. Take for example, when football powerhouse Michigan University was beat in 2007 by Appalachian State University, a little-known, former teacher's college. In the post-game interviews, the Appalachian State players spoke about their team—how they practiced together and played to support each other (WRAL, 2007). The Appalachian squad and coaches knew their own strengths as well as what the other team possessed. Appalachian State played with heart as well as technical expertise, and they achieved their goal of winning the game. Their interpersonal relationships and ability to work together as a team helped propel the Appalachian State players to victory.

Just as there is offense, defense, and special teams in football, schools have people with expertise. Like sports teams, schools have improvement goals, and in schools with strong relationships is a collective heart. In schools, relationship validation is more often in the halls and e-mails than on a scoreboard: Thank you. Your efforts are appreciated. You did an incredible job on ____!; I just wanted to check in with you. How is everything going?; I was thinking about your concern with ____.; I value your opinion. What do you think about____? All these statements are validating—they each convey that someone has taken notice of good works or to address a concern.

To offer another analogy, relationships are like plants in that they require tending. While some plants are more resilient than others, they all require some level of attention.

Words and actions have power. The speaker may have long forgotten affirming someone's efforts, but the employee is likely to remember. Likewise, when a teacher shares a concern that goes unaddressed, the educator may wonder if the administrator even cares. Throughout this book, ideas from the field provide examples of how to build, strengthen, and address relationships within four identified areas: vision, communication, team sense, and influence.

Vision

Leaders must be able to cast a vision and have the strength to pull in the net. They must know their organization, their followers, the larger community, and themselves. Leaders need to support faculty members in recognizing their current reality and discerning where they would like to go. The vision can provide the fuel for a school's success by setting a clear agenda for action, specifying what excellence and success are, and providing the direction for people to work proactively without heavy management (DuFour & Eaker, 1998). Motivated and energized faculty and staff proactively work with parents and community members to create an environment that facilitates student social and academic growth.

Many good leaders "act through their followers," and "a leader's behavior is successful because it is translated into the follower's actions," (Van Dick, Hirst, Grojean, & Wieseke, 2007, p. 134). In the process of pursuing their vision, school and department leaders build bridges between the current reality and the desired reality. Working toward a vision is like fishing: There are good days and challenging days, but the key to catching fish or to realizing a vision is to keep trying! Inadequate leadership can be detrimental to a school's efficiency because people have difficulty working hard for someone whom they do not respect or who does not seem devoted to the school's best interest.

Communication

Effective communicators are attuned to both what they say, how they say it, and what they look like when they are communicating. For example, if the principal is giving a welcome and highlighting the value of a professional development session for the entire faculty, and then the principal stays and participates in the session, he or she has demonstrated the importance of the session's topic. Even if the professional development is a flop, leadership's presence sends a supportive message that everyone is in this together.

Communication needs to be authentic to the individual leader—what works well for one colleague may feel awkward for someone else. Colleagues with established relationships with staff can often do more than someone just starting out. Leaders can enhance relationships such as when they engage in specific conversations about the teacher's students or follow up with a teacher who has been for a family emergency. These good communicators typically get more from their staff because can reach people on both a personal and professional level. They clearly articulate the desired outcome clear and outline the process to arrive at the outcome. In essence, communication is the bridge between one person and another.

Team Sense

Team sense is more than just knowing names and faces: It is about interactions with others. Capitalizing on strengths, addressing concerns, building capacity, and meeting needs are all components of team sense. From reducing staff's sense of vulnerability to involving teachers in the decision-making process to addressing staffing issues, leadership needs a strong sense of team in order to put the right person in the right place to get the job done. For some with well developed interpersonal skills, this aspect of relationship building comes easily. For others, deliberate actions and use of tools bridges the gap between procedural management and instructional leadership.

One principal likens team sense to being in a family. As the head of the family, she oversees everyone and makes deliberate choices as to how involved she becomes in their endeavors. Some may want or need more direction than others. To carry the family analogy one step further, coming into an established school is like marrying into the family. It takes time to develop the new relationships, and in the beginning it is often wise to be cognizant of how your actions may be perceived by others.

Influence

Many assume that influence comes hand in hand with leadership. However, influence is like respect in that it must be earned. Any leader can influence people to do things through fear or negative reinforcement. A clear example can be found in a children's tale about how to influence others. The sun and the wind are talking and a little boy wearing a rain jacket comes along. The wind tells the sun that it can blow the boy's jacket off. So, the wind blows a cold, strong wind. But the boy just holds the jacket even tighter. Then the sun takes a turn. It shines so brightly that the boy gets hot and throws off his jacket. The moral of this story is that gentle persuasion often wins out over forceful pressure.

School leaders influence teachers, parents, and students by example as well. They also influence their superiors, which earns them respect among their colleagues. The key to influence is the ability to establish positive relationships. A leader will have more influence if people perceive that the leader has integrity, is competent, and has the best interest of students at heart.

Leaders also have more influence *if they have the trust* of those with whom they work and also *if they trust* those with whom they work. For example, on the first day of school, teachers often receive all of their supplies in a box grade book, chalk or dry erase markers, sticky notes, pens, and paper clips. A teacher receives her box but knows she will need more paper clips because of how she will organize student folders for the year, so she goes to the supply closet and grabs another box. The principal is standing near the supply closet and asks, "Didn't you get a box of paper clips? Why do you need more?" What the teacher hears is "I don't trust that you will be a good steward of the supplies, and you are not professional enough to determine your supply needs." Before the school year even begins, the trust between the principal and the teacher is broken. If the principal operates the school building in this manner, she will have limited influence. The ripple effect of that little incident reverberates throughout the school year.

Recap

Author's Tale

A Combination of Personal and Professional Interactions Build Relationships

Judy Mahler is now retired with more than 30 years of administrative and teaching experience. Yet in 2001, I had the opportunity to observe her for a day as I completed some coursework for my doctorate. She adeptly cultivated relationships in her role as an instructional leader.

I recorded a sampling of her interactions with staff, and she demonstrated a focus on people and their needs when she:

- met with a teacher to discuss an upcoming observation
- provided feedback to a new teacher on an upcoming lesson
- addressed student achievement
- had a meeting about implementing a program to assist students who are visually impaired
- counseled a substitute teacher on how to obtain the information needed to become a licensed teacher

(Cont'd.)

> **Author's Tale** *(Continued)*
>
> Judy listened, provided targeted feedback or support as appropriate, and made the most of "chance interactions" with faculty, students, and others that she encountered as she moved throughout the school. People felt valued and affirmed by her. She inquired about how a teacher's spouse was doing as she recalled that the teacher was out the previous couple of days when her husband had surgery. This combination of personal and professional interactions builds good relationships in a school.
>
> Judy has some guidelines that help her relationships with staff, and they include the following:
>
> - Provide timely responses to people's inquiries, ideally before going home at the end of the day.
> - Foster growth in the profession (such as the talk with the substitute teacher).
> - Address critical staffing issues (for teachers who are having challenges in the classroom and need additional support).
> - *Make an effort to personally acknowledge people every day.*
>
> —Jenny Hindman

References

Adams, J. E. (2000). *Taking charge of curriculum: Teacher networks and curriculum implementation*. New York: Teachers College Press.

Alliance for Excellent Education. (2005). *Issue brief—Teacher attrition: A costly loss to the nation and to the states*. Washington, DC: Author. Retrieved from www.all4ed.org

Ärlestig, H. (2007, Spring). Principals' Communication Inside Schools: A Contribution to School Improvement? *Educational Forum, 71*(3), 262–273. Retrieved April 11, 2008, from http://web.ebscohost.com.proxy.wm.edu/ehost/pdf?vid=3&hid=4&sid=3f9858b4-4285-41f8-9b52-ccfda6abb3bd%40sessionmgr7

Ashley, B.(Summer 2008).The ABCs of strong leadership. *Air & Space Power Journal, 22*(2), 68–71, Retrieved July 01, 2008, from Expanded Academic ASAP via Gale: http://find.galegroup.com.proxy.wm.edu/itx/start.do? prodId= EAIM

Barkhi, R., Varghese, J., & Pirkul, H. (1999). An experimental analysis of face to face versus computer mediated communication channels. *Group Decision and Negotiation, 8*(4), 325–347. Retrieved April 11, 2008, from http://find.galegroup.com.proxy.wm.edu/itx/start.do?prodId=EAIM>

Billingsley, B. S. (2004). Promoting teacher quality and retention in special education. *Journal of Learning Disabilities, 37*(5), 370–376.

Bolman, L. G., & Deal, T. E. (1997). *Reframing Organizations* (2nd ed.). San Francisco: Jossey-Bass.

Buchen, I. H. (1998). Servant leadership: A model for future faculty and future institutions. *The Journal of Leadership Studies, 5*(1), 125–134.

Bryson, J. M. (1995). *Strategic Planning for Public and Nonprofit Organizations: A Guide to Strengthening and Sustaining Organizational Achievement* (2nd ed.). San Francisco: Jossey-Bass.

Campbell, K. S., White, C. D., & Johnson, D. E. (2003). Leader-member relations as a function of rapport management. *The Journal of Business Communication, 40*(3): 170–195. Retrieved on April 8, 2008, from http://find.galegroup.com.proxy.wm.edu/itx/start.do?prodId=EAIM

Camphire, G. (2001). Are our teachers good enough? *SEDLetter, 13*(2). Retrieved November 12, 2001, from http://www.sedl.org/pubs/sedletter/v13n2/1.htm

Charlotte Advocates for Education. (2004). *Role of principal leadership in increasing teacher retention: Creating a supportive environment.* Charlotte, NC: Author.

Cohen, A. R. & Bradford, D. L. (1990). *Influence without authority.* New York: Wiley.

Council of Chief State School Officers (2008). *Educational leadership policy standards: ISLLC 2008.* Washington, DC: CCSSO. Retrieved April 25, 2008, from http://www.ccsso.org/content/pdfs/elps_isllc2008.pdf

Cross, C., & Regden, D. W. (2002). Improving teacher quality. *American School Board Journal.* Retrieved May 17, 2002, from http://www.absj.com/current/coverstory2.html

Danielson, C. (2007). The many faces of leadership. *Educational Leadership, 65*(1), 14–19.

Darling-Hammond, L., & Berry, B. (n.d.). *Recruiting teachers for the 21st century: The foundation for educational equity.* Retrieved February 10, 2002. from www.teachingquality.org/pdf/recruitingteachersforthe21stcentury.pdf

Darling-Hammond, L. (2000). *Solving the dilemmas of teacher supply, demand, and standards: How we can ensure a competent, caring, and qualified teacher for every child.* New York: National Commission on Teaching & America's Future.

Day, C. (2005). Principals who sustain success: Making a difference in schools in challenging circumstances. *International Journal of Leadership in Education, 8*(4), 273–290. Retrieved April 24, 2008, doi:10.1080/13603120500330485

Dexter, R., & Turk, R. (2002). Research. *Journal of School Improvement, 3*(2). Retrieved on September 6, 2007, from www.ncacasi.org/jsi/2002v3i1/research

Dinham, S. (2005, November). *Principal leadership for outstanding schooling outcomes in junior secondary education.* Presentation at the Australian Association for Research in Education, Parramatta, Austrialia. Retrieved October 16, 2007, from http://www.aare.edu.au/05pap/din05528.pdf

Dinham, S. (2007). How schools get moving and keep improving: Leadership for teacher learning, student success and school renewal. *Australian Journal of Education, 51*(3), 263–276. Retrieved July 01, 2008, from Expanded Academic ASAP via Gale: http://find.galegroup.com.proxy.wm.edu/itx/start.do?prodId=EAIM

Donaldson, G. A. (2007). What do teachers bring to leadership? *Educational Leadership, 65*(1), 26–29.

Douglas, C., & Zivnuska, S. (2008). Developing trust in leaders: An antecedent of firm performance. *SAM Advanced Management Journal, 73*(1), 20–29. Retrieved July 01, 2008, from Expanded Academic ASAP via Gale: http://find.galegroup.com.proxy.wm.edu/itx/start.do?prodId=EAIM

DuFour, R. & Eaker, R. (1998). *Professional learning communities at work: Best practices for enhancing student achievement.* Bloomington, IN: National Educational Service.

Duke, D. L., Tucker, P. D., Salmonowicz, M. J., & Levy, M. K. (2007). How comparable are the perceived challenges facing principals of low performing schools? *International Studies in Educational Administration, 35*(1), 3–21.

Edwards, V. B. (Ed.). (2000). *Quality counts 2000.* Bethesda, MD: Education Week.

Emrich, C. G., Brower, H. H., Feldman, J. M., & Garland, H. (2001). Images in words: Presidential rhetoric, charisma, and greatness. *Administrative Science Quarterly, 46,* 527–557.

Farling, M. L., Stone, A. G., & Winston, B. E. (1999). Servant leadership: Setting the stage for empirical research. *The Journal of Leadership Studies, 6*(1/2), 49–72.

Friedkin, N.E., & Slater, M.R. (1994). School leadership and performance: A social network approach. *Sociology of Education 67*(2), 139–157.

Fullan, M. (2001). *Leading in a culture of change: Being effective in complex times.* San Fransciso, CA: Jossey-Bass.

Fullan, M., Bertani, A., & Quinn, J. (2004). New lessons for districtwide reform. *Educational Leadership, 61*(7), 42–46.

Genzuk, M. (1997). Diversifying the teaching force: Preparing paraeducators as teachers. *ERIC Digest #96-2.* Washington, DC: ERIC Clearinghouse on Teaching and Teacher Education (ERIC Document Reproduction Service No. ED406362)

Gersten, R., Keating,T., Yovanaf, P., & Harniss, M. K. (2001). Working in special education: Factors that enhance special educators' intent to stay. *Exceptional Children, 67*(4), 549–567.

Glascock, C. H., & Taylor, D. (2001). The elementary principal/superintendent relationship as perceived by teachers and its effects on the school: A case study comparison. *Education Policy Analysis Archives, 9*(45). Retrieved June 2, 2008, from http://epaa.asu.edu/epaa/v9n45.html

Glatthorn, A.A. (2000). *The principal as curriculum leader: Shaping what is taught and tested* (2nd ed.). Thousand Oaks, CA: Corwin Press.

Greenleaf, R. (1970). *Servant as leader.* Newton Center, MA: Robert K. Greenleaf Center.

Hallahan, K. (2000). Enhancing motivation, ability, and opportunity to process public relations messages. *Public Relations Review 26*(4), 463. Retrieved April 10, 2008, from http://find.galegroup.com.proxy.wm.edu/itx/start.do?prodId=EAIM

Hallinger, P., & Heck, R. H. (1998). Exploring the principal's contribution to school effectiveness: 1980–1995. *School Effectiveness and School Improvement, 9*(2), 157–191. Retrieved September 6, 2007, from Education Research Complete at http://search.ebscohost.com/login.aspx?direct=true&db=ehh&AN=5701490&site=ehost-live

Harris, K. J., & Kacmar, K. M. (2006). Too much of a good thing: The curvilinear effect of leader-member exchange on stress. *The Journal of Social Psychology, 146*(1), 65–80. Retrieved September 25, 2007, from find.galegrou.com.proxy.wm.edu/itx/infomakr.do?&contentset-IAC-documents&type=retrieve&tabID=t002&prodID=EAIM&docID=A142722049&source=gale&srcprod=EAIM&usergroupname=viva_wm&version=1.0

Harris, S. (2004). *BRAVO principal: Building relationships with actions that value others*. Larchmont, NY: Eye on Education.

Hart, S. L., & Quinn, R. E. (1993). Roles executives play: CEOs, behavioral complexity, and firm performance. *Human Relations 46*(5), 543–75. Retrieved on April 8, 2008 from http://find.galegroup.com.proxy.wm.edu/itx/retrieve.do?

Hattie, J. (2003, October). *Teachers make a difference: What is the research evidence?* Background paper presented at the 2003 ACER Research Conference, Melbourne, Australia. Retrieved March 30, 2005, from www.acer.edu.au

Herzberg. F. (1966). *Work and the nature of man*. Cleveland, OH: World.

Hirsch, E. (2006). *Recruiting and retaining teachers in Alabama: Educators on what it will take to staff all classrooms with quality teachers*. Hillsborough, NC: Center for Teaching Quality.

Hoy, W. K., & Miskel, C. G. (2001). *Educational administration: Theory, research, and practice* (6th ed.). New York: McGraw-Hill.

Hoy, W. K., & Woolfolk, A. E. (1993). Teachers' sense of self-efficacy and the organizational health of schools. *The Elementary School Journal, 93*(4), 355–373.

Huffman, J. B., & Hipp, K. A. (2000, April). *Creating communities of learners: The interaction of shared leadership, shared vision, and supportive conditions*. Paper presented at the annual meeting of the American Educational Research Association, New Orleans, LA. Retrieved October 23, 2008 from http://eric.ed.gov/ERICWebPortal/custom/portlets/recordDetails/detailmini.jsp?_nfpb=true&_&ERICExtSearch_SearchValue_0=ED452582&ERICExtSearch_SearchType_0=no&accno=ED452582

Ingersoll, R. M. (2001). *Teacher turnover, teacher shortages, and the organization of schools* (Document R-01-1). Seattle: University of Washington, Center for the Study of Teaching and Policy.

Inman, D., & Marlow, L. (2004). Teacher retention: Why do beginning teachers remain in the profession? *Education, 124*(4), 605–614.

Johnson, S. M., & The Project on the Next Generation of Teachers. (2006, Summer). Why new teachers leave...and why new teachers stay. *American Educator*. Retrieved October 19, 2006 from http://www.aft.org/pubs-reports/american_educator/issues/summer06/Teacher.pdf

Jorgenson, O., & Peal, C. (2008, March). When principals lose touch with the classroom. *Principal, 87*(4), 52–55. Retrieved April 11, 2008, from Education Research Complete database: http://web.ebscohost.com.proxy.wm.edu/ehost/pdf?vid=3&hid=115&sid=985b04ca-52e1-449f-baf6-56b240ff6ec0%40sessiongr102

Jorissen, K. T. (2002). 10 things a principal can do to retain teachers. *Principal Leadership, 3*(1), 48–54.

Killion, J. (2005). The code: Turning teammates into team players. *JSD, 26*(2). Retrieved December 23, 2006, from www.nsdc.org/library/publications/jsd/killion262.cfm

King, P. (2007). 2007 NFL Preview: Peyton Manning. *Sports Illustrated, 107*(9), 74–77.

Kouzes, J. M., & Posner, B. Z. (2002). *The Leadership Challenge* (3rd ed.). San Francisco, CA: Jossey-Bass.

Kouzes, J. M. & Posner, B. Z. (1993). *Credibility: How leaders gain and lose it, why people demand it*. San Francisco: Jossey-Bass.

Krüger, M., Witziers, B., & Sleegers, P. (2007, March). The impact of school leadership on school level factors: Validation of a causal model. *School Effectiveness & School Improvement, 18*(1), 1–20. Retrieved April 24, 2008, doi:10.1080/09243450600797638

Lee, C., & Zemke, R. (1993). The search for spirit in the workplace. *Training, 30*(6), 21–29.

Leech, D., & Fulton, C. R. (2008). Faculty perceptions of shared decision making and the principal's leadership behaviors in secondary schools in a large urban district. *Education, 128*(4), 630–645. Retrieved July 01, 2008, from Expanded Academic ASAP via Gale: http://find.galegroup.com.proxy.wm.edu/itx/start.do?prodId=EAIM

Leithwood, K., & Jantzi, D. (1999). The relative effects of principal and teacher sources of leadership on student engagement with school. *Educational Administration Quarterly, 35*, 679–706.

Lewis, L. K. (2006). Employee perspectives on implementation communication as predictors of perceptions of success and resistance. *Western Journal of Communication 70*(1), 23–47. Retrieved on April 8, 2008, from http://find.galegroup.com.proxy.wm.edu/itx/start.do?prodId=EAIM.

Mackey, B., Pitcher, S., & Decman, J. (2006). The influence of four elementary principals upon their schools' reading programs and students' reading scores. *Education, 127*(1), 39–55. Retrieved April 24, 2008, from Academic Search Premier database.

Madlock, P. E. (2008).The link between leadership style, communicator competence, and employee satisfaction. *The Journal of Business Communication 45*(1), 61–88. Retrieved on April 8, 2008, from http://find.galegroup.com.proxy.wm.edu/itx/start.do?prodId=EAIM

Matheson, A. S., & Shriver, M. D. (2005). Training teachers to give effective commands: Effects on student compliance and academic behaviors. *School Psychology Review, 34*(2), 202–220. Retrieved September 23, 2005, from Expanded Academic ASAP. Thomson Gale. http://find.galegroup.com.proxy.wm.edu/

Mayfield, J.,& Mayfield, M.(2006). The benefits of leader communication on part-time worker outcomes: a comparison between part-time and full-time employees using motivating language. *Journal of Business Strategies 23*(2), 131–154. Retrieved April 11, 2008, from http://find.galegroup.com.proxy.wm.edu/itx/start.do?prodId=EAIM

McEwan, E. K. (2003). *7 steps to effective instructional leadership* (2nd ed.). Thousand Oaks, CA: Corwin Press.

McKechnie, J. L. (Ed.). (1983). *Webster's new twentieth century dictionary.* New York: Simon and Schuster.

Mehrabian, A. (1981). *Silent messages: Implicit communication of emotions and attitudes.* Belmont, CA: Wadsworth.

Merriam-Webster Online. Retrieved September 14, 2007, from http://www.m-w.com/dictionary/cultivate

Metropolitan Life. (2006). *The MetLife survey of the American teacher: Expectations and experiences.* Retrieved October 13, 2006, from www.metlife.com/teacher survey

Morrow, P. C., Yoshinori, S., Crum, M. R., Ruben, R., & Pautsch, G. (2005). The role of leader-member exchange in high turnover work environments. *Journal of Managerial Psychology, 20*(8), 681–694. Retrieved September 25, 2007, from Expanded Academic Index ASAP. Find.galegroup.com.proxy.wm.edu/itx/start.do?proid=EAIM

Newstrom, J. W., & Davis, K. (1997). *Organizational behavior: Human behavior at work.* New York: McGraw-Hill.

Nohria, N., Groysberg, B., & Lee, L. (2008). Employee motivation: A powerful model. *Harvard Business Review, 86*(7/8), 78–84.

Otto, S. J., & Arnold, M. (2005). A study of experienced special education teachers' perceptions of administrative support. *College Student Journal, 39*(2), 253–259.

Paglin, C. (2000). The good humor man. *Northwest Education Magazine, 5*(3). Retrieved December 23, 2006, from www.nwrel.org/nwedu/spring00/goerke.html

Peery, A. B. (2004). *Deep change: Professional development from the inside out*. Lanham, MD: Scarecrow Education.

Perie, M., Baker, D. P., & Whitener, S. (1997). *Job satisfaction among America's teachers: Effects of workplace conditions, background characteristics, and teacher compensation* (NCES 97-XXX). U.S. Department of Education, Office of Educational Research and Improvement, National Center for Education Statistics. Washington, DC: U.S. Government Printing Office. Retrieved November 21, 2001, from www.nces.ed.gov/pubs97/07471.pdf

Pigge, F. L., & Marso, R. N. (1996). *Academic aptitude and ability characteristics of candidates teaching and not teaching five years after graduation*. Paper presented at the annual meeting of the American Educational Research Association, New York. (ERIC Document Reproduction Service No. ED402270)

Quinn, T. (2005). Principal's impact on teacher retention. *Academic Exchange, 9*(2), 225–229.

Richbell, S., & Ratsiatou, I. (1999). Establishing a shared vision under total quality management: Theory and practice. *Total Quality Management, 10*(4 & 5), S684–S689.

Robinson, V. M., & Timperley, H. S. (2007). The leadership of the improvement of teaching and learning: Lessons from initiatives with positive outcomes for students. *Australian Journal of Education, 51*(3), 247–263. Retrieved July 01, 2008, from Expanded Academic ASAP via Gale: http://find.galegroup.com.proxy.wm.edu/itx/start.do?prodId=EAIM

Rowe, M. B. (1972). *Wait time and rewards as instructional variables, their influence in language, logic, and fate control*. Chicago, IL: National Association for Research in Science Teaching. (ERIC ED 061103)

Schmoker, M. (2006). *Results now: How we can achieve unprecedented improvements in teaching and learning*. Alexandria, VA: Association for Supervision and Curriculum Development.

Senge, P. (2006). *The fifth discipline: The art and practice of the learning organization*. New York: Doubleday.

Sergiovanni, T. J. (1992). *Moral leadership: Getting to the heart of school improvement*. San Francisco, CA: Jossey-Bass.

Sharbrough, W. C., Simmons, S. A., &. Cantrill, D. A. (2006). Motivating language in industry: Its impact on job satisfaction and perceived supervisor effectiveness. *The Journal of Business Communication 43*(4), 322–344. Retrieved on April 8, 2008, from http://find.galegroup.com.proxy.wm.edu/itx/start.do?prodId=EAIM.

Sias, P. M. (2005). Workplace relationship quality and employee information experiences. *Communication Studies, 56*(4), 375–395. Retrieved September 25, 2007, from Expanded Academic Index.

Smith, P. G. (2001). Communication holds global teams together. *Machine Design, 73*(14), 70–74.

Smithers, A., & Robinson, P. (2003). *Factors affecting teachers' decisions to leave the profession*. Centre for Education and Employment Research, University of Liverpool, Research Report No. 340, Retrieved June 2, 2008, from http://www.dfes.gov.uk/research/data/uploadfiles/RR430.pdf

Snyder, T. D., Dillow, S. A., & Hoffman, C. M. (2007). *Digest of Education Statistics 2006* (NCES 2007-017). National Center for Education Statistics, Institute of Education Sciences, U.S. Department of Education. Washington, DC: U.S. Government Printing Office.

Sparks, D. (2005). Principals partner with supervisors, teacher leaders. *Results*. Retrieved September 6, 2007, from *www.nsdc.org/library/publications/results/res12-04spar.cfm*

Statt, D. A. (1994). *Psychology and the world of work*. Washington Square, NY: New York University Press.

Stronge, J. H. (2008). *Qualities of effective principals*. Alexandria, VA: Association for Supervision and Curriculum Development.

Supovitz, J. A. (2000). Translating teaching practice into improved student achievement. In S. H. Fuhrman (Ed.), *From the capitol to the classroom: Standards-based reform in the states*. Chicago: University of Chicago Press.

Texas Center for Educational Research. (2002). *The cost of teacher turnover*. Austin, TX: Author.

Truckenbrodt, Y. B. (2000). The relationship between leader-member exchange and commitment and organizational citizenship behavior. *Acquisition Review Quarterly, 7*(3), 233–239. Retrieved September 25, 2007, from Expanded Academic Index ASAP at http://find.galegroup.com

Tschannen-Moran, M. (2004). *Trust Matters*. San Francisco: Jossey-Bass.

Tschannen-Moran, M., & Hoy, A. W. (2001). Teacher efficacy: Capturing an elusive concept. *Teaching and Teacher Education, 17*(7), 783–805.

Van Dick, R., Hirst, G., Grojean, M., & Wieseke, J. (2007). Relationships between leader and follower organizational identification and implications for follower attitudes and behaviour. *Journal of Occupational & Organizational Psychology, 80*(1), 133–150. Retrieved April 24, 2008, from Academic Search Premier database.

Votey, S. (2002). Getting Help: Heading the small school. *Independent School, 62*(1), 57. Retrieved September 6, 2007, from Professional Development Collection database at http://search.ebscohost.com.proxy.wm.edu/login.aspx?direct=true&db=tfh&AN=8672850&site=ehost-live

Wald, J. L. (1998). *Retention of special education professionals: A practical guide of strategies and activities for educators and administrators.* National Clearinghouse for Professions in Special Education, The Council for Exceptional Children, Reston, VA. (ERIC Document Reproduction Service No. ED 422691)

Wenglinsky, H. (2002). How schools matter: The link between teacher classroom practices and student academic performance. *Educational Policy Analysis Archives, 10*(12). Retrieved February 28, 2002, from http://epaa.asu.edu/epaa/v10n12/

Whitworth, J. (2000, March). Preparing, recruiting, and retaining special education personnel in rural areas. In J. Lemke (Ed.) *Capitalizing on Leadership in Rural Special Education: Making a Difference for Children and Families*, Conference Proceedings, Alexandria, VA. (ERIC Document Reproduction Services No. ED 439893)

Wise, A. E., Darling-Hammond, L., & Berry, B. (1987). *Effective teacher selection from recruitment to retention.* Santa Monica, CA: Rand. Retrieved September 6, 2007, from http://www.rand.org/pubs/reports/2005/R3462.pdf

Wood, S., & Huffman, J. (1999). Preventing gang activity and violence in schools. *Contemporary Education, 71*(1), 19. Retrieved September 6, 2007, from Professional Development Collection database at http://search.ebscohost.com.proxy.wm.du/login.aspx?direct=true&db=tfh&AN=3440659&site=ehost-live

WRAL. (2007). *ASU-Michigan Quotes.* Retrieved on September 6, 2007, from www.wral.com/sports/story/1768930/?print_friendly=1

For Product Safety Concerns and Information please contact our EU representative GPSR@taylorandfrancis.com
Taylor & Francis Verlag GmbH, Kaufingerstraße 24, 80331 München, Germany

www.ingramcontent.com/pod-product-compliance
Lightning Source LLC
Chambersburg PA
CBHW081422230426
43668CB00016B/2318